CIVIL WAR *in* TEXAS *and*
NEW MEXICO TERRITORY

CIVIL WAR
in TEXAS and
NEW MEXICO
TERRITORY

Steve Cottrell

Illustrated by Andy Thomas

PELICAN PUBLISHING COMPANY
Gretna 1998

The word "Pelican" and the depiction of a pelican are trademarks
of Pelican Publishing Company, Inc., and are registered
in the U.S. Patent and Trademark Office.

Library of Congress Cataloging-in-Publication Data

Cottrell, Steve.
    Civil War in Texas and New Mexico territory / by Steve Cottrell ;
illustrated by Andy Thomas.
        p.   cm.
    Includes bibliographical references and index.
    ISBN 1-56554-253-3 (pb)
    1. Texas—History—Civil War, 1861-1865.   2. New Mexico—
History—Civil War, 1861-1865.   3. United States—History—Civil
War, 1861-1865—Participation, Hispanic American.   I. Title.
E532.C68   1997
973.7'08968—dc21   97-6464
                                                                  CIP

Manufactured in the United States of America
Published by Pelican Publishing Company, Inc.
1101 Monroe Street, Gretna, Louisiana 70053

This book is respectfully dedicated to all the brave men on both sides who fought for what they believed in during the war in the far West, 1861-1865—especially the nearly forgotten Hispanic soldiers: men who served the Union in forces such as the New Mexico volunteers under Lt. Col. Manuel Chaves and those who served the South in units such as the irregular Confederate cavalry of Col. Santos Benavides. They experienced the tragedy of the American Civil War firsthand, struggling in battle to help forge the nation we have today. The often-ignored Hispanic heroes of the War Between the States should not be forgotten. They too are part of America's heroic heritage.

Contents

Acknowledgments

In the mid-1980s, I listened to my friend and fellow reenactor, Bill Fannin, spin yarns around our campfire at Fort Scott National Historic Site in Kansas. The outrageous tale of Paddy Graydon's exploding mules at Valverde, New Mexico, made an impression on me. The interest sparked that night has finally resulted in this little volume of adventure stories.

I am also indebted to park ranger Steve Weldon and the excellent research library at Wilson's Creek National Battlefield, Republic, Missouri. Also, I am grateful for the help I received from my great-uncle, Rex Lawson, who provided additional source material. A special thanks to Andy Thomas whose excellent artwork has doubled the value of this book. And I appreciate the photography provided by Don Montgomery, historian at Prairie Grove Battlefield State Park in Arkansas, and Bob Tommey of Carthage, Missouri. Last but not least, my wife Rhonda Rae deserves more than a big hug for her help on the word processor.

CIVIL WAR *in* TEXAS *and* NEW MEXICO TERRITORY

CHAPTER 1

Lone Star Rebels

Hazy clouds of gunsmoke rolled slowly across the dry Texas prairie. As the sulfurous fog gradually lifted, a ghastly scene of carnage was revealed: a score of lifeless bodies lay scattered about in the dust. Texas horsemen rode around the corpses, inspecting the results of their surprise attack on Ochoa's band of ruffians. Most of the Mexican banditos had been wiped out in the deadly fusillade of gunfire, but Ochoa himself had escaped across the border with a few of his followers. After Ochoa had hung a county judge and issued his challenge to Confederate authority, Texas justice had been swift and merciless. Irregular cavalry, sent by Col. John ("Rip") Ford, had caught up with Ochoa's gang at a nameless, godforsaken battleground somewhere north of the Rio Grande. The date was April 1, 1861, eleven days before Fort Sumter, South Carolina, was fired upon—and the Civil War in Texas had already begun.

Young, proud, and independent, the state of Texas never backed away from a fight. When war came, her people immediately jumped into the middle of the fray as if it were merely a rollicking saloon brawl. At the time, few realized what a long, devastating struggle the war would be. Between sixty and seventy thousand Texans volunteered to fight for the Confederate cause.

It was probably only natural that Texas would side with her

sister states of the South. Her economy and social structures reflected Southern ways, although much of her population's frontier lifestyle was a bit rougher than that of her eastern counterparts. However, not all Texans believed their state should leave the Federal Union. As a matter of fact, Sam Houston himself adamantly opposed secession.

Houston was governor of Texas at the time the state legislature authorized a convention to discuss secession. Despite Houston's attempts to rally support for the United States, the delegates defied their proud old leader and voted 171-6 to secede from the Federal Union on February 2, 1861. In a general election held on February 23, the citizens of Texas voted overwhelmingly to validate the convention's ordinance of secession. Then on March 2, Texas Independence Day, the convention reconvened and passed a motion uniting Texas with the Confederate States of America. Denounced as a traitor by many of his fellow Texans, Sam Houston was forced to vacate the governor's office on March 16. The legendary hero sadly retired to Huntsville, dishonorably discharged from public service. Lt. Gov. Edward Clark then assumed the office of governor.

Meanwhile, eager young volunteers rallied under three newly appointed Texas colonels: Benjamin McCulloch, his brother Henry, and John S. Ford. All three were illustrious men of action; Indian fighters, Texas Rangers, as well as veterans of the Texas Revolution and Mexican War. Back in 1836, young Ben McCulloch had narrowly missed accidentally killing his commander, Gen. Sam Houston, at the Battle of San Jacinto when Houston carelessly rode in front of a loaded cannon which McCulloch was about to fire. John "Rip" Ford earned his nickname by writing "R.I.P." at the bottom of casualty lists during the 1846-1848 Mexican War.

The McCulloch brothers and Ford had been commissioned by a fifteen-man board called the Committee of Public Safety, which had been given the task of preparing for war by the Secession Convention (even before the validation election). The commanders' first objective was to capture all Federal

Col. Ben McCulloch

Col. Rip Ford

installations and armaments in Texas. They wasted no time in carrying out their orders. At dawn on February 16, Ben McCulloch boldly rode into San Antonio with a thousand raw recruits armed with shotguns, squirrel rifles, pistols, and Bowie knives. The rough-cut horsemen surrounded various U.S. government buildings in town including the historic shrine to Texas valor, the Alamo Mission, which had become a Federal quartermaster depot. Elderly Major General David Twiggs, a Georgia-born Southern sympathizer who was the commander of all U.S. troops and posts in Texas, offered no resistance and willingly surrendered everything to Col. McCulloch. Confederates gathered around the Alamo in a boisterous celebration as the U.S. flag was lowered and replaced by the Lone Star banner.

Meanwhile, Henry McCulloch secured the surrender of all Federal posts in North Texas while Rip Ford seized the U.S. installations in the southern part of the state. By March 20, all Federal forts in Texas had fallen into Confederate hands without a single casualty on either side.

After the initial takeover of Federal installations, there was some confusion concerning what to do with captured U.S. troops. Although some were at first threatened with captivity as prisoners of war, it soon became Texas policy to allow the soldiers to march out of the state since at that time there had been no formal declaration of war. Thus the San Antonio garrison, a detachment of the 8th U.S. Infantry Regiment, marched out of the city with their weapons on their shoulders and their flags flying proudly as their band played patriotic tunes.

One perplexed U.S. officer who stepped off an army wagon into a San Antonio street just as the city came under Confederate control was none other than a gentleman named Robert E. Lee. Lee was a lieutenant colonel who had been in command of the 2nd U.S. Cavalry Regiment stationed at Fort Mason. He had recently received orders to report to Washington, D.C., for reassignment. There he was to meet with General-in-Chief Winfield Scott. Lee had stopped over in San Antonio to board a stagecoach which would take him out of

Texas on his long journey back East. He received a hostile reception in the city when three secessionist army commissioners threatened to detain him unless he declared himself in favor of their cause. Lee boldly discounted the threat and stated that he was a Virginian, not a Texan, and would decide for himself which side to take. Fortunately for Lee, the commissioners chose to not press the issue and allowed him to continue on his journey. Thus Lee narrowly avoided becoming a prisoner of war in a Confederate detention camp and went on to Washington, where Gen. Scott offered him the top field-command position in the Union Army. Of course, Lee made his historic decision at that point in time, profoundly affecting the course of American history. Perhaps the war would have been much shorter had the Texans taken the future Confederate commander prisoner.

After the capture of all U.S. posts in Texas and the resulting withdrawal of Federal troops, settlements in the state suddenly became vulnerable to their foes: hostile Native American warriors and Mexican bandits (such as Ochoa's gang). Therefore two mounted regiments of eager new recruits were assigned the task of defending the state. Volunteers of the 1st Texas Mounted Rifles under Col. Henry McCulloch were sent to the northwest border, reoccupying abandoned posts and patrolling the region for Indian war parties. The 2nd Texas Mounted Rifles, commanded by Col. Rip Ford, scoured the southern border, defending settlers from Ochoa and other Mexican raiders. Ford sent his second in command, Lt. Col. John R. Baylor, to defend the southwestern portion of the border along the Rio Grande. Baylor was a fiery Indian fighter who had recently engaged in the newspaper publishing business, expressing his supremacist political sentiments in a journal entitled *The White Man.*

On April 11, the Confederate government established an official Department of Texas and placed Colonel Earl Van Dorn at its head, dispatching him to San Antonio to take command. The forty-year-old West Pointer had already established

Lt. Col. John Baylor

a heroic reputation in Texas. Before the war, he had led the U.S. Cavalry against hostile warriors of the Comanche Tribe in the region, becoming a household word around many a settler's family fireplace. Orders given to Van Dorn included the directive to intercept U.S. troops attempting to leave the state of Texas. Unfortunately, this directive nullified previous Texas policy to allow safe passage of U.S. troops from the state and resulted in the capture of several hundred Federal soldiers, who became prisoners of war. One bitter U.S. officer pointed out the irony of having defended Texas settlers for years only to be imprisoned by those same citizens. Most of these soldiers were detained for nearly two years in squalid camps before being exchanged for Confederate prisoners. Fortunately for the South, former U.S. Army officer Robert E. Lee had already reached Richmond and was not a prisoner of war in Texas.

Near the end of spring, Col. Van Dorn ordered Lt. Col. Baylor to guard against a possible Federal invasion from U.S. troops still stationed at forts on the upper Rio Grande in New Mexico Territory. Baylor was given authority to take the offensive if he wished, and the aggressive white supremacist jumped at the chance to march against Federal troops. Having occupied El Paso and Fort Bliss, Baylor made plans to forcibly take Fort Fillmore, 40 miles to the north across the New Mexico border.

At the time, New Mexico Territory included all of the present-day states of New Mexico and Arizona. The Federal government had appointed a territorial governor, Abraham Rencher, and had assigned Colonel Edward R.S. Canby to command the military Department of New Mexico. Canby, at his headquarters in Santa Fe, busied himself with preparing his forces for defense rather than offense. This was the logical course since a great deal of the settlers in New Mexico Territory were Southern sympathizers. Citizens in the town of Mesilla, only six miles from Ft. Fillmore, were already flying the Confederate flag when news reached Canby's headquarters that Baylor's battalion of the 2nd Texas Mounted Rifles had occupied El Paso and appeared ready to invade the territory. Canby, a quiet, tall, effi-

Col. Edward Canby

cient officer, reinforced Ft. Fillmore and placed its 700-man force under the command of a thirty-four-year veteran of the U.S. Infantry, gray-bearded Major Edward Lynde. Canby also requested that Gov. Rencher issue a call for volunteers to defend the territory from Confederate invasion.

On July 23, Lt. Col. Baylor led 250 Texas troops across the border into New Mexico and rode north along the Rio Grande River. The hot, dusty, Confederate horsemen camped within only 600 yards of Ft. Fillmore on the night of the 24th. A surprise attack on the adobe post was planned for daybreak. However, during the night one of Baylor's pickets (perimeter guards) deserted and made his way into the Union fort, warning Major Lynde and his men of the impending assault. Baylor's men heard the drums sounding within Ft. Fillmore and Union troops could be seen manning the post's defenses. Wisely, Baylor called off the attack since he had lost the element of surprise. Instead, he and his men rode into Mesilla and received a warm welcome from the town's citizens.

That afternoon at 3:00 P.M., elements of the 7th U.S. Infantry, supported by a small force of mounted riflemen, marched out of Ft. Fillmore and advanced upon the town. Baylor's small Confederate force hastily took cover on rooftops and behind a long adobe wall enclosing a corral. When the U.S. troops were about 500 yards from the nearest town structures, Lynde halted their march and sent two men forward with a white flag and a message for Baylor demanding his unconditional surrender. In a reply reminiscent of the Texas Revolution of 1836, Baylor defiantly responded that if Lynde wanted the town and the Texas troops holding it, he would have to " . . . come and take them."

The Yankee major accepted the challenge and grimly ordered his battery of three howitzers forward. He gave the command to open fire and his artillerymen nervously rammed their loads down the cannons' stocky, bronze barrels. With thunderous, fiery salvos, the big guns hurled several shells in the direction of their foes. The fearsome, whirling missiles exploded much too high over their targets to cause any damage. The inglorious fireworks display brought forth jeers and mocking laughter from the Texans as well as from a number of townsfolk who watched the spectacle from their rooftops. Meanwhile the Union infantry maneuvered into position through tall cornstalks on both sides of the sandy road where the artillery stood. Then Major Lynde ordered his three companies of mounted rifles forward to lead the attack on Mesilla. A bugle sounded and the horsemen started forward at a trot. But before they broke into a full gallop, the Texans opened fire from behind their wall. Several men and horses went down in dusty, thrashing heaps. The heavy gunfire turned back the charge as the mounted troopers retreated beyond the ranks of the Union infantry. They had lost one killed and three wounded. The Confederates continued to blast away with their rifles, shotguns, and muskets as billowing clouds of gunsmoke rolled from their firing line behind the adobe wall. Two Union artillerymen fell dead at their guns and three other Yanks bit the dust with gunshot wounds. Suddenly, to the surprise of both sides, Major Lynde ordered a withdrawal from the field, announcing it was too late in the day to continue the action. The Yanks retreated back to the safety of their fort with three dead and six wounded. The Texans, with no casualties at all, cheered wildly as they watched their foes march away.

The brief but violent exchange of gunfire apparently convinced Major Lynde that he faced a stronger force than his own. In reality, the Yanks outnumbered the Texans by almost three to one, yet their fifty-five-year-old commander simply panicked at the thought of being overwhelmed by the enemy. His spies had informed him that Confederate reinforcements were on the march, including the necessary artillery to lay siege to the fort. Incredibly, Lynde decided to abandon Ft. Fillmore and retreat to Fort Stanton, 140 miles across the desert to the northeast! During the chaotic preparations to abandon Ft. Fillmore, it is said that some rowdy soldiers broke into the post's ample supply of "medicinal" whiskey and filled their canteens.

Texans at Mesilla repelled the U.S. assault.

It was not the best beverage to have on hand during a grueling march across the arid desert.

At 1:00 A.M. on July 27, Major Lynde's troops marched out of Ft. Fillmore with their artillery and baggage wagons lumbering along behind them. The fires they had set within the abandoned outpost struggled to remain alive as the flames died out in the partially gutted adobe buildings. The retreating force made good progress during the night's mild weather along the sandy road. However, when the unmerciful desert sun arose, it didn't take long for the July heat to take its toll on Lynde's column of thirsty, sweat-drenched soldiers. Their water supply was severely limited. When the road began to climb upward toward San Augustin Pass in the mountain foothills, the miserable military column began to break apart in disorder. Troops were strung out along the road for miles. Major Lynde's most critical objective soon became the water hole at a wayside spring five miles beyond the pass.

By this time, Lt. Col. Baylor was in full pursuit of the retreating U.S. force. It didn't take long for the Confederate cavalrymen to catch up with their foe's baggage train, easily capturing Lynde's wagons and howitzers without a shot being fired. Beyond San Augustin Pass, Baylor's men encountered heat-exhausted U.S. infantrymen lining the road for five miles and begging for water. Finally, as Baylor's mounted troopers came within sight of the spring, Major Lynde frantically attempted to form his men in line of battle. Only about 100 Yanks slowly reached for their weapons and half-heartedly prepared to defend their position. The rest languished miserably around the spring, ready to surrender. It was obvious to everyone, including Lynde, that Baylor had already won. Soon a limp, white cloth arose from the demoralized mass of men at the spring.

Lt. Col. Baylor, despite his fire-eating political views and eagerness to fight the U.S. government, proved himself to be a gracious victor. After allowing Lynde and his men to recuperate for two days at the spring, he paroled them all. Under a parole agreement (utilized primarily early in the war), prisoners were sent home after giving their word of honor not to fight again until official notification that the other side had received an equal number of parolees. Before letting Lynde's troops trudge off to freedom, Baylor let his defeated foes have a total of fifty old, but workable, carbines with enough ammunition to defend themselves if they encountered hostile Indians.

Other Federal forces in New Mexico Territory, which had been marching to reinforce Ft. Fillmore, received word of Lynde's surrender and immediately changed direction, heading for Fort Craig, 100 miles farther north. Learning of the Union disaster, the U.S. commander at Ft. Stanton, where Lynde had hoped to seek refuge, abandoned his post as well and marched his troops northwest all the way to Albuquerque and Santa Fe. Awaiting reinforcements in Mesilla, Col. Baylor triumphantly issued a proclamation on August 1, establishing a new Confederate territory called Arizona, including all of New Mexico south of the 34th parallel. Baylor declared himself to be governor and Mesilla to be the capital.

Meanwhile, the war was heating up in Texas itself. Besides skirmishing with banditos such as Ochoa's gang and clashing with hostile Indians, Confederates finally exchanged gunfire with U.S. forces. A Union ship, ironically named USS *South Carolina*, had arrived in Galveston Bay as a representative of the U.S. blockade force. On August 3, the ship moved closer to the mainland and came within range of Confederate artillery. A brisk duel took place between the ship and a shore battery. The only casualties were civilian bystanders on shore: one man was killed and several boys were wounded. Since the arrival of the *South Carolina* in the bay about four weeks earlier, nearly a dozen ships attempting to "run the blockade" had been captured or destroyed. However, there were a great many more ships that had successfully entered and left Galveston's harbor during the same month-long time period.

By this time, Texas troops were beginning to show up in different theaters of the war, marching to far-away battlefields. As a matter of fact, Ben McCulloch had been promoted to the rank of brigadier general and was in command of not only Texas troops but also Arkansas, Missouri, and Louisiana soldiers that comprised the entire Confederate army at the Battle of Wilson's Creek, Missouri, on August 10, 1861. It was the second-largest battle of the first year of the American Civil War. McCulloch emerged victorious, even though his Texas cavalry under Col. Elkanah Greer was severely shot up during a futile charge against the Federal artillery and infantry defending "Bloody Hill." The Union commander at Wilson's Creek, Brig. Gen. Nathaniel Lyon, was shot out of his saddle, becoming the war's first Union general to be killed in action. As for McCulloch, the fifty-year-old former Texas Ranger made newspaper headlines across the nation with his victory in Missouri. Already Texas was making a fighting name for itself in the war.

Taking note of the impressive abilities of Texas fighting men, President Jefferson Davis was persuaded to issue orders for another army to be raised in Texas to conquer all of New Mexico Territory for the Confederacy. Because of the recent military success in the Southwest, the Confederacy now had high hopes of extending its domain even farther west to include California, Nevada, Colorado, and elsewhere. But first, the entire New Mexico Territory would have to be secured. Destined to lead this dramatic campaign of westward expansion was an old career soldier who had devised the entire plan himself and personally presented it to President Davis. His name was already immortalized in military circles due to the success of his army bivouac inventions. The Sibley tent and Sibley stove were used widely by both sides in countless camps across the continent. Brigadier General Henry H. Sibley had styled his ideal military tent after the Indian teepee lodge, but he had simplified its cone-shaped design for easy transport by the use of only one center pole and a handy little stove with which to safely heat the roomy, canvas structure. Sibley was a rough-cut old West Pointer whose classmates at the academy decades earlier had ironically included Edward Canby, who now would prove to be

Brig. Gen. Henry Sibley

a formidable foe in New Mexico. Gen. Sibley was a veteran of the Seminole War in Florida and the Mexican War as well, but his better days of professional soldiering were behind him by the time he resigned from the U.S. Army to join the Confederate cause. It was no secret that the old warrior's fondness for hard liquor had made him, in the words of a contemporary, a "walking whiskey keg."

While Colonel (or Governor) Baylor continued to hold his position at Mesilla, General Sibley raised three regiments of mounted volunteers at San Antonio. By October 1861, his force was 3,500 strong and included artillery surrendered by Twiggs (who incidentally was now a Confederate major general with his headquarters in New Orleans). On October 22, Sibley's little army rode out of San Antonio amid the cheers of admiring citizens. Their destination, Fort Bliss, was nearly 700 miles away. To allow the precious waterholes along the way to replenish them, the troopers had to travel in small detachments, crossing the arid desert of west Texas with minimal losses.

Thus the fateful year of 1861 came to a close with the Confederacy defiantly strong. The new nation seemed to be able to hold its own in any fight, whether it be in Texas, New Mexico Territory, Missouri, or Virginia.

CHAPTER 2

Desert Empire

By January 1, 1862, General Sibley had assembled most of his invasion force at Fort Bliss, Texas. On the crisp, wintry day of January 3, he ordered his army to cross the border into New Mexico Territory. His immediate destination was an abandoned post on the Rio Grande known as Fort Thorn, located northwest of Mesilla. There the Confederate troops would wait for about a month, in light snow, for the last detachments to join them before the campaign could get into full swing. Disease, alcohol consumption, and sheer boredom would become problems at Fort Thorn, as was the case at all frontier posts on both sides during the war. However, the tedious camp routine was occasionally interrupted by a nighttime horse stealing raid by Apaches, followed by a spirited chase and a few parting shots fired into the darkness.

On February 7, Sibley's army rode out of Fort Thorn and marched up the Rio Grande Valley to meet its destiny. By this time, the Confederate force was only 2,515 strong; some of the original 3,500 had already been lost to pneumonia, smallpox, and dysentery. Also, Sibley had left a force of 630 men under Colonel William Steele to protect the region of Mesilla and had sent a detachment of 54 men farther west to occupy Tucson.

Riding through high winds filled with sleet and snow, the tough little Confederate army consisted of the 4th, 5th, and 7th

Regiments of Texas Mounted Volunteers (unofficially referred to by the men themselves as the 1st, 2nd, and 3rd Regiments of the "Sibley Brigade"). Also present was a battalion of six companies from Col. Baylor's force and a new unit of rough and rowdy frontier volunteers who called themselves the "Company of Brigands." Sibley also had fifteen pieces of artillery, a long wagon train of supplies, and a herd of cattle. Riding upriver in detachments, the "Sibley Brigade" planned to rendezvous about 70 miles north, in front of its first objective—Fort Craig.

An impressive frontier stronghold, Ft. Craig consisted of twenty-two adobe and rock buildings, surrounded by a thick adobe and earthen wall with firing holes for riflemen. Col. Canby had rushed as many reinforcements to the post as he could and by early February, the fort's defenders numbered 3,810. Only 1,200 of them were U.S. Army regulars; the rest were volunteers and militiamen. The regulars consisted of elements of the 5th, 7th, and 10th Infantry Regiments and several companies of the 1st and 3rd Cavalry. Canby's eight artillery pieces were manned by two companies of his cavalry.

The best volunteer unit camped at Ft. Craig was the 1st New Mexico Volunteer Regiment. It consisted of ten companies of well-trained, mounted frontiersmen, many of them Hispanics, and was commanded by none other than the already famous Western scout and adventurer, Kit Carson. Carson had been commissioned a lieutenant colonel of U.S. volunteers when the war broke out. He had become a legend in his own time, largely due to the widely read accounts of the Western explorations of John C. Fremont, for whom Carson had served as chief scout. Carson's life had been one long series of adventures: fur trapping, exploring, scouting, Indian fighting, and now—commander of an entire Union regiment in the Civil War. Other volunteer units camped around Ft. Craig were elements of the 2nd, 3rd, 4th, and 5th New Mexico Volunteers; about a thousand members of various New Mexico militia groups; the "Company of Scouts," which consisted mainly of barroom rowdies recruited by a saloon keeper named James "Paddy" Graydon (who had at one time been a member of a regiment of U.S. Dragoons); and last but not least, the "Colorado Volunteers" under Captain Theodore H. Dodd, a company of miners and frontiersmen from Colorado who had rushed to Ft. Craig in response to Canby's urgent request for reinforcements.

On February 16, 1862, the 5th Texas Mounted Volunteers arrived a mile from Ft. Craig in the stark desert of New Mexico Territory. However, Col. Canby chose to hold his forces at the stronghold and not be lured out into the open by the Rebel cavalrymen. He hoped to mow down the Confederates as they launched futile assaults against the fort's powerful defenses. But General Sibley realized that Ft. Craig was too strong for a head-on assault and decided to simply bypass the post. He planned to cross the east bank of the Rio Grande, march about six miles north, recross the river upstream at Valverde, then continue his march north to Albuquerque. This strategy would leave Col. Canby's troops isolated, cut off from their supply line.

Waiting two days for a sand storm to die out, Sibley forded the Rio Grande on February 19. On the afternoon of February 20, Canby received word of the Confederate movement and realized exactly what Sibley was up to. Canby knew he had no choice but to intercept the Confederates, so he marched most of his force east of Ft. Craig. Rough terrain with sandy ridges and ravines slowed his progress and made maneuvers especially difficult for his artillery. Nevertheless, he caught up with his foes and for a time the two opposing forces eyed each other as they moved along parallel ridges. Finally, the Confederates managed to lob some artillery shells in the midst of the 2nd New Mexico Volunteers and panicked their horses, as well as the riders. The resulting cavalry stampede spread to other units. As dusk approached, Canby ordered most of his forces back to the fort, leaving behind a small detachment of infantry to guard the west side of the river.

That night Union Captain Paddy Graydon and some of his saloon buddies from the Company of Scouts tied boxes full of howitzer shells to a couple of aged pack mules. Their scheme was to stampede the Confederate cattle herd, depriving their foes of fresh beef. Quietly leading the animals across the river in the moonlight, Graydon and his men lit the fuses and whipped the mules' hindquarters, sending the poor, miserable creatures toward the Texas longhorns. Suddenly the confused old critters turned and trotted back toward Graydon and his surprised comrades. The terrified volunteers scurried back to their own lines, racing to keep ahead of their four-legged pursuers. Finally, at a safe distance behind Graydon's men, the shells exploded with a thunderous roar. The distant explosions only slightly startled the drowsy Confederate cattle herd but relieved the Union "scouts" who had gone to so much trouble to put a couple of elderly pack animals out of their misery.

Early the next morning, the Confederates were on the march again, heading up the east side of the Rio Grande. Col. Canby ordered a detachment of Yanks to hasten up the west bank and block the Texans from crossing the ford at Valverde. When the Federals arrived, they discovered an advance unit of 180 Rebel cavalrymen in a cottonwood grove on the east riverbank. The Texas troopers were commanded by a well-known cattle rancher and Mexican War veteran, Major Charles L. Pyron. Soon, four companies of regular U.S. Cavalry splashed across the shallow river and assaulted Pyron's men, driving the Southerners back in a flurry of gunfire. The Confederates took up a new defensive position at some nearby sand hills as the Federals unlimbered two artillery batteries on the west bank. The big guns began to blaze away at their foes across the stream as more of Gen. Sibley's brigade galloped onto the scene and deployed for action. The Battle of Valverde had begun.

The action heated up quickly as Lieutenant Colonel William Scurry, a popular Texas politician, arrived on the field with his 4th Texas Mounted Volunteers and a battery of howitzers. During the ensuing artillery duel, Scurry attempted to retake the cottonwood grove in a futile counterattack. Around noon, Union reinforcements arrived, including Col. Kit Carson and

Paddy Graydon's plan backfires.

his men along with the Colorado Volunteers under Capt. Theodore Dodd. The reinforcements moved upstream to flank the Southern force. However, they had trouble finding a suitable place to cross, finally fording the chilly stream in four feet of water. Shivering, soggy infantrymen, including the hardy Colorado troops, "fixed bayonets" and charged into a small stand of woods held by dismounted Texas troopers. The Rebels fled and the jubilant Yanks marched out of the tree line, reforming their ranks with bayonets gleaming in the sun.

Suddenly to their front, a battle line of Confederate cavalry galloped forward. Two companies of the 5th Texas Mounted Volunteers were "lancers" armed with outdated, but fearsome-looking, nine-foot-long poles tipped with one-foot-long, three-inch-wide steel blades. Each weapon was decorated with a red pennant and looked quite impressive to a foe when it was pointed in his direction. One company of over fifty lancers under Captain Willis Lang now came full speed at the Colorado Volunteers, who nearly panicked at the deadly sight. But their commander, Capt. Dodd, sternly closed up his ranks and shouted to his men, "They are Texans. Give them hell!" And they did. Two rifle volleys brought down numerous men and horses in tangled masses as others reached the line of bayonets only to be impaled by cold steel.

Interestingly, there were only a few cases of hand-to-hand combat in the Civil War in which the bayonet actually came into physical contact with the enemy on a mass scale. This was one such case. An eyewitness account tells of Texas cavalrymen being literally lifted out of their saddles by Colorado bayonets. Of the lancers who made the dramatic charge at Valverde, only three survived unharmed.

Meanwhile, the command structure on both sides changed as the battle grew to major proportions. Col. Canby arrived from Ft. Craig about 3:00 P.M. to take personal field command of the Union army as the action raged. Behind the Confederate lines, Gen. Sibley became ill and retired to the rear in an ambulance. Some claimed he had downed too much whiskey

Charge of the Fifth Texas lancers

but such allegations were never proven. Before leaving the action, Sibley put a very able officer in charge. Colonel Thomas Green of the 5th Texas Mounted Volunteers was a respected veteran of the Texas Revolution whose men reputedly would follow him anywhere. Now he was field commander of the entire Confederate force in the first major battle of the New Mexico Campaign.

Col. Canby was in the process of repositioning his troops for a flank attack on his foes when Col. Tom Green launched two major Confederate assaults. As the various Union units attempted to get realigned according to Canby's orders, 250 mounted Texans charged the Federal right flank in order to capture a battery of artillery on the southern end of the battle-field. The oncoming Rebels were repulsed after various Yankee units rushed to the rescue, including Kit Carson's 1st New Mexico Volunteers. However, the frantic scramble to force back the

Confederate charge, as well as the failure of the 2nd New Mexico Volunteers to move into position, left the center of the Union line totally vacant. As a result, there were no Union units to be shifted from the center to the left flank, where the main Confederate attack occurred, about a mile north of the previous assault. A determined force of 750 dismounted Texas troopers suddenly came roaring into the Union left from behind a ridge of sand hills. Led by Major Samuel Lockridge, the Confederates' main objective was a Federal artillery battery under Capt. Alexander McRae.

Two battalions of regulars as well as two companies of militia assigned to defend the artillery were unable to stop the furious Texas onslaught. Capt. McRae himself was shot dead at one of his guns, as was Maj. Lockridge; some claim they shot each other. Col. Canby ordered forward his reserves, two companies of U.S. Cavalry regulars, but their charge was to no avail against the Confederate juggernaut. Then four infantry companies under Capt. Benjamin Wingate double-timed across the smoky battlefield to attempt to retake McRae's guns. They only succeeded in getting themselves shot up, with Wingate himself mortally wounded. Through the swirling mixture of gunsmoke and desert dust, Kit Carson saw the disaster developing in the distance and started some of his own command toward the raging scene, but they were too far away to rescue the doomed Union left wing. Exasperated, Canby ordered a general retreat back to Ft. Craig before the dauntless Texans could flank his entire force. As the Federals splashed back across the Rio Grande, artillery shells from McRae's captured guns exploded mercilessly around them.

Col. Green's victorious little army was preparing to cross the river in pursuit of their fleeing foes when a Union messenger rode up with a white flag. Col. Canby was requesting a truce to recover his dead and wounded. The chivalrous Col. Green agreed to the truce and the Confederate pursuit was canceled. The Battle of Valverde was over. Exact casualties are debatable: Canby reported only 68 Federals killed, 160 wounded, and 35 missing, while Green reported just 36 Confederate dead, 150 wounded, and only 1 missing. Some historians believe the true casualties in the fierce little battle on the Rio Grande would have to be greater than what the commanders reported, both sides trying to downplay their losses as minimal.

The Confederates had paid dearly for their victory, not only in the loss of men but also in supplies and horses. Numerous wagons had been burned and broken with a great loss in food, ammunition, and equipment. So many cavalry mounts had been killed that Col. Scurry's entire 4th Regiment had to be converted to a dismounted unit—in effect, infantry. Meanwhile, at Ft. Craig, Col. Canby and many of his regular U.S. Army officers were quick to point the finger of blame at the New Mexico militia units, who became scapegoats for the Federal defeat at Valverde. Thus racism raised its ugly head at the fort since most troops and many officers of the militia units were Hispanics, such as the 2nd New Mexico Volunteers under the command of Col. Miguel Pino. Such allegations were cruelly unfair, for many Hispanics had fought bravely and paid a heavy cost in blood for the Federal cause. For example, Col. Carson's Hispanic troops of the 1st New Mexico Regiment had done their duty with a courage second to none.

On February 22, the day after the battle, Gen. Sibley had regained his health and was again in command. He sent a delegation of officers to Ft. Craig under a white flag to demand the post's surrender. Col. Canby angrily refused and prepared to defend his fort. No doubt he hoped the Texans would assault the powerful walls so he could emerge victorious. But Gen. Sibley was smarter than that and resorted to his original plan: bypass Ft. Craig, cutting its supply line, and march north to Albuquerque.

On February 23, Gen. Sibley marched his army north, leaving the Valverde battlefield and Ft. Craig behind. Ironically, Col. Canby chose to remain at Ft. Craig for basically the same reason Sibley chose to bypass the post: to cut the enemy supply line. By staying at the fort, Canby not only planned to block

Hispanic soldier

Confederate supplies and reinforcements from Texas, but he also hoped to eventually trap Sibley between his force and the sizable reinforced Union garrison at Ft. Union. The Federal force at Ft. Union, northeast of the territorial capital at Santa Fe, now became the major obstacle for Sibley to overcome before conquering New Mexico Territory for the Confederacy.

On February 25, about two hundred Hispanic militiamen under Col. Nicolas Pino attempted to make a stand against Sibley's vanguard at the town of Socorro. However, when the Texans wheeled up an artillery piece and opened fire, the defiant militiamen had little choice but to surrender or be blown to smithereens. Sibley's march north continued as Maj. Charles Pyron led the way with a battalion that included the rowdy "Company of Brigands." The Brigands soon made a reputation for themselves as ruthless pillagers, plundering civilian homes along the route of march.

Meanwhile on March 1, the Federal troops in Albuquerque withdrew to Santa Fe after loading as many supplies as possible into wagons and setting fire to all government buildings containing other provisions. The next morning, Pyron's battalion entered the town and promptly salvaged as many supplies as possible for the Confederate army, which was already in need of food. About 60 miles west of Albuquerque at the village of Cubero, Confederates were able to seize a good stockpile of muskets, ammunition, and foodstuffs intended for Federal use on campaigns against hostile Indians. Another fortunate gain for Sibley's hungry brigade, which by now was encamped in and around Albuquerque, was the capture of a U.S. Army wagon train loaded with supplies intended for Ft. Craig. Resupplied, Sibley's force again pushed north as Federal troops evacuated the capital of Santa Fe on March 4 in the same manner they left Albuquerque, attempting to deny the Texans as many provisions as possible. One hundred and twenty U.S. Army wagons, loaded with Federal supplies and escorted by all the Union troops from Santa Fe and Albuquerque, rushed to Ft. Union, 85 miles to the northeast. The territorial governor also left, moving his government and records to the village of Las Vegas near Ft. Union.

Gen. Sibley's New Mexico Campaign had thus far been a stunning military success for the Confederacy. A rapid push farther northward by the Texans at this critical time would have possibly secured the entire territory for the South. Colorado, with its rich gold mines, would have been vulnerable to a Confederate invasion. However, the Sibley Brigade lumbered along slowly. Not until March 13 was the Confederate flag finally raised over the old Palace of the Governors in Santa Fe. By that time, Federal reinforcements had arrived at Ft. Union from Colorado Territory, spoiling for a fight.

Nine hundred and fifty men of the 1st Colorado Volunteer Infantry Regiment under Colonel John P. Slough, a Denver lawyer, had made a grueling forced march through freezing weather and mountainous terrain. They had made it to Ft. Union on March 11, having marched over 400 miles in only thirteen days. The imperious and aristocratic Col. Slough claimed seniority over Ft. Union's commandant, Colonel Gabriel Paul, and assumed command of the entire post. Slough himself was not popular with his own troops due to his abrasive personality. As a matter of fact, some of his men harbored pure hatred for him. There had even been talk of an assassination plot.

With the arrival of Slough's tough Colorado troops, the Federal force was now over 1,400 strong. In addition to the "Pike's Peakers," as some called the Coloradans, the Union force was made up of army regulars and New Mexico militiamen. Slough wasted no time in going on the offensive. Despite orders from Col. Canby to defend Ft. Union, Slough marched out of the post on March 22 with 1,342 troops and eight cannon. His force consisted of his own 1st Colorado Regiment, a company of the 2nd Colorado Volunteers under Captain James H. Ford, a battalion of the 5th U.S. Infantry, a detachment of the 1st and 3rd U.S. Cavalry, a company of the 4th New Mexico Volunteers, and two artillery batteries of four guns each commanded by

The Colorado troops marched through harsh, freezing mountains to Fort Union.

Captain John F. Ritter of the 5th Infantry and Lieutenant Ira W. Claflin of the 3rd Cavalry. Slough left behind Col. Paul and a mere handful of men to defend Ft. Union.

Col. Slough's column advanced southwest on the Santa Fe Trail as a portion of the Sibley Brigade moved ahead of the main Confederate force on the same route. The opposing armies were destined to clash on the historic trail where it winds through the southern tip of the Sangre de Cristo Mountains. It is the region known as Glorieta Pass: a meandering roadway lined with rocky slopes and scattered pine trees.

On the afternoon of March 26, the vanguard of Slough's force, 418 infantry and cavalry, descended the western slope of Glorieta Pass and surprised a scouting patrol of thirty-two Texans, capturing them all without a fight. The Union vanguard's commanding officer, Major John M. Chivington, learned from his prisoners that the vanguard of the Confederate army, about four hundred troops under Maj. Charles Pyron, was not far ahead. The bearded Chivington was a blustering, barrel-chested officer over six feet tall who had been a fire-and-brimstone preacher in Denver before enlisting to carry an avenging sword against the Rebels. Upon learning of the nearby enemy force, the aggressive Chivington ordered his men forward at the double-quick toward a narrow valley at the west end of Glorieta Pass known as Apache Canyon. As the Yanks rounded a bend in the road, they came face to face with a detachment of Maj. Pyron's command, a column of Texas cavalry with two artillery pieces.

The Texans unlimbered their six-pounder field guns (cannon capable of firing six-pound balls) and began blasting away at the surprised Colorado troops, who immediately withdrew out of range of the murderous shells. However, bull-roaring Maj. Chivington rallied his troops and ordered his infantry and a detachment of dismounted cavalry to climb the rough, pine-and cedar-covered slopes that lined the road in order to flank his foe. The Texans were soon forced to pull back by the intense gunfire of the hill-climbing riflemen. They retreated about a mile and a half into Apache Canyon. Joined by the rest

DECISIVE ACTIONS
at
Glorieta Pass
and
APACHE CANYON

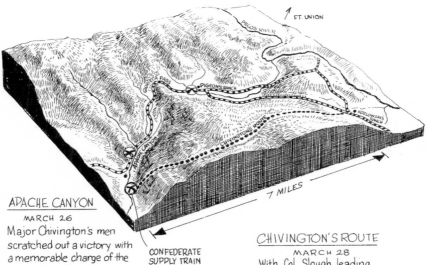

FT. UNION

PECOS RIVER

GLORIETA PASS

PIGEON'S RANCH

KOZLOWSKI'S RANCH

CHIVINGTON'S ROUTE

APACHE CANYON

7 MILES

CONFEDERATE SUPPLY TRAIN

APACHE CANYON
MARCH 26
Major Chivington's men scratched out a victory with a memorable charge of the Colorado Volunteer Cavalry.

PIGEON'S RANCH
MARCH 28
In several hours of vicious fighting, Confederate troops forced the Federals to retire from the field of battle.

CHIVINGTON'S ROUTE
MARCH 28
With Col. Slough leading the main attack in Glorieta Pass, Major Chivington led a detachment over the hills and captured the Confederate supply train.

Maj. John Chivington

of Maj. Pyron's force, the Texans crossed a log bridge over a 15-foot-wide gully, destroyed it, and unlimbered their artillery again at a bend in the road. Then Pyron, copying his opponent's tactic, deployed some of his troops up the steep, rocky hills on both sides of the canyon. As Chivington and his troops advanced, they came under the heavy gunfire of Pyron's entire Confederate force. The stubborn Chivington ordered troops up the sides of the canyon again, competing with the Texans for a higher vantage point. Meanwhile, the fighting preacher himself rode fearlessly among the rest of his troops on the road with a pistol in each hand, bellowing commands and directing the volley fire of his infantrymen.

Firing their rifles and carbines from behind boulders and stunted cedar trees, the Yanks on the rocky slopes gradually forced back their Rebel foes as Chivington ordered a cavalry charge below on the canyon road. A company of mounted Colorado troopers galloped forward in a whirlwind of dust toward the Texan artillery battery. The fierce horsemen plunged into the gully near the smoldering ruins of the log bridge. Down one side and up the other, the blue-coated troopers and their wild-eyed horses emerged from the shallow gorge, peppered by shot and shell. Boldly they rode on with upraised sabers in their relentless charge. Confederate rifles on the canyon slopes blazed away at them while to their front, more rifles as well as artillery did the same. But there seemed to be no stopping the Pike's Peakers, who miraculously rode through the deadly gauntlet of gunfire to crash headlong into their foes, furiously slashing with their heavy sabers in a war-crazed frenzy. The Texans gave way and began a fighting retreat, somehow managing to successfully limber their two cannon in the chaos and wheel the big guns safely to the rear before they could be captured.

Chivington pursued Pyron, who stubbornly resisted his advance until nightfall when the fighting finally fizzled out. Union losses were five killed, fourteen wounded, and three missing. Confederate casualties are unknown, but Chivington reported taking seventy-one prisoners. A Texan messenger

The fearless cavalry troopers plunged into the gully.

under a white flag arrived at the Federal camp that night with Pyron's request for permission to recover his dead and wounded. Chivington, encamped at a ranch near the middle of Glorieta Pass, a good distance from the battlefield, agreed to a truce until 8:00 A.M. the next day. The mean skirmish at Apache Canyon was the first Union victory in New Mexico Territory.

During the night, Maj. Pyron anxiously awaited reinforcements as he prepared to defend his new position at the western end of Glorieta Pass against a possible morning attack by the tenacious Federal force. The Confederates were now fully aware of the presence of Colorado troops. To meet the threat, Col. William Scurry made a 16-mile forced march from Galisteo through freezing nighttime temperatures with about seven hundred Texans to unite with Pyron's force. Meanwhile, Maj. Chivington had withdrawn his troops to the far eastern end of Glorieta Pass to Kozlowski's Ranch, where there was an ample water supply for his force. There he awaited the arrival of the main Union column under Col. John Slough. The day passed with neither side moving to attack the other. However, both forces swelled in numbers as reinforcements arrived. Col. Scurry took overall command of approximately a thousand Confederates camped at Johnson's Ranch, while Col. Slough commanded over thirteen hundred Federals at Kozlowski's Ranch. Thus the stage was set for a deadly showdown the following day.

On the morning of March 28, Col. Scurry and his battle-ready Texans marched into the western end of Glorieta Pass, leaving eighty supply wagons at Johnson's Ranch with a small guard force. Likewise, Col. Slough marched into the eastern end of the pass, but not with his entire force. He boldly split his little army, sending over a third of his men (about 490 troops) under Maj. Chivington on an off-road route over the mountain wilderness straight west. According to the plan, Chivington would then enter the western end of Glorieta Pass behind his foe to strike at the rear of the Confederate force. Chivington's column was guided by Lieutenant Colonel Manuel Chaves and his New Mexico volunteers, Hispanic militiamen who knew the land well. Meanwhile Col. Slough, with the rest of his men, marched on toward the center of Glorieta Pass. There he stopped to rest his troops and allow them to fill their canteens at a location known as "Pigeon's Ranch." The cluster of adobe buildings was named for its fun-loving owner's comical pigeon-like dance that he performed at social festivities.

The Union troops had just broken ranks at the ranch and started to relax when the brassy sound of bugles called them back to formation. Confederates had been spotted only about 800 yards ahead, moving through a grove of scrubby timber. It was 11:00 A.M. and the Yanks advanced only about 500 yards before they came under artillery fire. Col. Scurry had sent three cannon far out in front of his main Confederate force with his skirmishers. The Texans unlimbered their artillery on a ridge overlooking the Union position. Col. Slough halted his advance and formed a long, blue battle line across the valley. At the same time, he sent a detachment of cavalry forward to reconnoiter his foe's position. The cavalry was soon forced back to the Union line as the incessant crackle of distant rifle fire grew heavier. Col. Slough, on horseback, strained his eyes to observe the Confederate positions through his field glasses. Clouds of white gunsmoke billowed from the three-gun Texan battery as it blasted holes in the long line of Union troops, who re-formed and held their position with iron discipline. Slough ordered two companies of troops to climb the wooded, rocky slopes on the right and left in an effort to flank the Texans.

Meanwhile, Col. Scurry deployed his dismounted cavalry in a long Confederate battle line with Maj. Pyron commanding the right, Major Henry Raguet the center, and himself personally in charge of the left. Scurry was soon faced with a Union advance on his left flank as Colorado troops attempted to move forward, under cover of an old irrigation ditch, to seize the deadly Texan artillery battery that had plagued them since the battle began. Scurry's troops charged across the field and into the ditch, driving back the Coloradans in a savage hand-to-hand struggle. At the same time, Maj. Pyron advanced and successfully flanked the Union left as Maj. Raguet applied continuous pressure in the center. Col. Slough then ordered a Union withdrawal to a new position on the perimeter of Pigeon's Ranch. There he established a new battle line as his artillery skillfully provided covering fire.

The Texan artillery moved up to new positions, hastily unlimbered their guns, and commenced firing. A thunderous artillery duel began as the troops on both sides redeployed. Slough's howitzers got the correct range on a Confederate battery and scored a direct hit on one gun, as the barrage continued with fiery thunderclap explosions shrouded in swirling clouds of smoke and dust. The Union artillery soon won the duel and nearly silenced all the Confederates' big guns. Yet Col. Scurry, despite his lack of artillery support, launched several furious head-on charges against the Union troops, some of whom had taken cover behind a long adobe wall and a series of corral fences. Hundreds of Texans surged forward as their high-pitched Rebel yells echoed through the canyon. Five times they charged the Union line and five times they were driven back. Finally they attempted a sixth charge, hurling themselves into a murderous storm of shot and shell as rifles and cannons blazed away at them. The Texans wavered and the Federals countercharged with bayonets. Again, intense hand-to-hand combat ensued. Maj. Pyron's horse was shot out from under him and Maj. Raguet was mortally wounded. Col. Scurry, his face bloodied by two grazing shots, ordered a withdrawal back to the Confederates' main line position.

Meanwhile, the Southern troops had fared better on the rocky slopes on the Union's right flank. Enfilading fire from Texans on the high ground once again forced the Federal artillery and infantry to pull back to a new position, this time east of Pigeon's Ranch. Scurry then advanced his entire force. Once more the Confederates charged the new Union battle line, and again brave young Texans fell before the blazing Colorado guns.

Although the Federals had beaten back this final Confederate assault, they had taken a severe pounding throughout the day. Col. Slough was shaken not only by the six hours of battle with Scurry's troops, but also by an obvious attempt by some of his personal enemies (within his own regiment) to assassinate him by aiming a volley in his direction during the battle. Exhausted, Slough wondered what had become of Chivington and his men. Why hadn't they galloped onto the battlefield in a glorious rear attack, surprising and trapping the Texas army? Instead, Slough had had to fight the battle without Chivington and his men, pummeled by a numerically superior force for six straight hours.

Giving up on Chivington's arrival, Slough finally ordered a retreat back to Kozlowski's Ranch. Gradually, various Union units withdrew as the gunfire died out, leaving the Texans in possession of the battlefield. Col. Scurry reported Confederate losses at Pigeon's Ranch to be thirty-six killed and sixty wounded. Col. Slough reported Union losses to total eighty-three killed and wounded. About twenty-five Confederates had been taken prisoner by the Federals. Most historians believe the casualty total for both sides was definitely higher than official reports indicate.

As the demoralized Federal force trudged toward Kozlowski's Ranch, a Confederate army ambulance flying a white flag caught up with the dusty blue column. Inside the wagon was the assistant adjutant of Gen. Sibley's army, Major Alexander Jackson, with a request for a truce to care for the dead and wounded. Col. Slough promptly agreed to a cease-fire, which took effect immediately and was to last until noon of the following day. The real reason behind the Confederate request became known about 10:00 P.M., as Maj. Chivington's column finally rode into the Federal camp with electrifying news. Chivington's troops, guided by Lt. Col. Chaves' Hispanic scouts, had reached the western end of Glorieta Pass by crossing 16 miles of mountain wilderness. There they arrived at the edge of a 200-foot-high bluff overlooking the entire Confederate supply train of about eighty wagons at Johnson's Ranch near

The Colorado troops lowered themselves down the bluff by ropes.

Apache Canyon. After lowering themselves down the steep hill with ropes, Chivington's troops surprised the small force left to guard the supply train, rapidly driving the outnumbered Texans away in a flurry of gunfire.

The Federals then proceeded to destroy every supply wagon, burning the Confederates' ammunition, food, clothing, saddles, tents, blankets, and medical supplies. In short, everything the Texans needed to survive in their New Mexico Campaign was consumed by flames. About half a mile from the supply train, the Federals also found 500 horses and mules corralled in a ravine. Most were Confederate cavalry mounts; all were destroyed. As Chivington's men completed their work of devastation, a Texan courier rode out from the canyon, observed the horrific scene of destruction, and galloped back up the canyon to carry the news to Col. Scurry.

As the sky above Johnson's Ranch darkened with the black smoke of Scurry's blazing wagon train, occasionally accented with the lightning flash of exploding ammunition, Chivington chose to return by the same route from which he came. In one amazing, dramatic strike, the fighting preacher and his troops had utterly crushed Confederate plans for a western empire. Instead of the Federals facing another defeat in New Mexico Territory, they emerged from the day's fire and fury with a smashing victory.

The tired and hungry Texans left their wounded behind at Pigeon's Ranch and, with nearly all their troopers without horses, withdrew to Santa Fe on foot. There they were reunited with the rest of the Confederate army: six companies of the 5th Texas under Col. Green and Gen. Sibley himself, who resumed personal command of his entire brigade. In a panic, Sibley fired off a communiqué to the governor of Texas requesting swift reinforcements. The Confederates confiscated everything they could find in the New Mexico capital, including horses, wagons, ammunition, and a good supply of Federal blankets intended for distribution to the Navajo Tribe.

Meanwhile at Ft. Craig, Col. Canby was unaware at this time

of the great success of Col. Slough's expedition. He only knew that Slough had disobeyed his orders by leaving Ft. Union. Canby sent a courier with orders for Slough to return immediately to Ft. Union with his force. Ironically, Slough now faced the possibility of a court-martial from Canby. Disgusted with the whole situation, and distrustful of his own men, Slough angrily sent off a letter of resignation and headed back to Denver to resume his law practice. Maj. Chivington then took full command of Slough's force and reluctantly marched his troops toward Ft. Union in compliance with Canby's orders.

Canby himself started north from Ft. Craig with 1,210 men on April 1. The Federal commander had been promoted to brigadier general just the day before. When Gen. Canby reached Socorro, 30 miles north of the post, he learned of the tremendous Union success at Glorieta Pass and immediately altered his plans. He sent orders to Col. Paul, commandant of Ft. Union, to march southwest toward Santa Fe and Albuquerque. Chivington, promoted to colonel, and his Pike's Peakers were to accompany Paul and his force. Meanwhile Canby would continue his march north, link up with Paul and Chivington, and drive the crippled Texan army out of New Mexico Territory.

When Gen. Sibley learned of Canby's advance north, he swiftly abandoned Santa Fe and rushed south to reach Albuquerque before the Federals. For it was in that adobe town that the precious remainder of the Confederate supplies were stored. This enabled Paul and Chivington to retake the territorial capital of Santa Fe without firing a shot. Paul, Chivington, and Canby then linked up as planned, 15 miles northwest of Albuquerque at Tijeras. The combined Union force now numbered 2,400 troops. The situation for the Texans looked grim. They were now outnumbered and didn't even have enough ammunition to last through a full day of battle. Sibley's request for reinforcements had gone unanswered. The gruff, hard-drinking old general knew he was licked. He had little choice but to retreat back to Texas.

The year 1862 had indeed taken a sour turn for the Lone

Star Confederates. Not only was their New Mexico Campaign falling apart, but Texas had also just lost a couple of their most talented leaders. Gen. Ben McCulloch had been shot out of his saddle by a Yankee sharpshooter at the Battle of Pea Ridge, Arkansas, on March 7. Another notable Texan, Gen. Albert S. Johnston, had also been killed, at Shiloh, Tennessee, on April 6. Still another Texan leader, Lt. Col. John Baylor, Confederate governor of the territory from which Sibley was now retreating, fell not by a bullet, but by the administrative actions of none other than President Jefferson Davis himself. Baylor had been struggling to put an end to Apache raids in his domain in the Messilla Valley. He sent an explosive order to the commander of a citizen militia known as the Arizona Guards outlining a brutal plan to kill all Apache warriors who would show up to negotiate a treaty. The controversial letter became public and caused a political scandal in Richmond, since President Davis had been trying to win over the tribes of Indian Territory (in present-day Oklahoma) as military allies.

In early 1862, Davis removed the politically incorrect Baylor from the governorship. Ironically, over a decade later, a similar assassination plot would be concocted by Modoc Indians dealing with the U.S. Army. Their victim was none other than Edward R. S. Canby, by then the commanding general of U.S. troops in the so-called Modoc War of 1873. At a pre-arranged negotiation parley with Modoc leaders, their chief, "Captain Jack," whipped out a revolver and shot Canby to death. Thus ended the career, and life, of the man who drove Sibley's Texans out of New Mexico Territory.

On April 12, Sibley's army evacuated Albuquerque and started their march south down both sides of the Rio Grande. The Confederates' shortage of artillery ammunition and draft animals to pull cannon made some of their big guns useless. Before leaving town, they buried eight howitzer barrels in a corral to keep them from the Federals. Initially, Gen. Sibley planned to overwhelm Kit Carson's small garrison force at Ft. Craig on his march south in order to capture the large stockpile of supplies stored at the post. However, Canby's maneuvers near the town of Peralta were to alter Sibley's plans drastically.

After midnight on April 15, Gen. Canby's army quietly deployed in the darkness on two sides of a Confederate encampment on the northern outskirts of Peralta. Col. Green's 5th Texas Regiment was camped in the fields around the home of the Federal territorial governor. While the enlisted men caught up on some badly needed rest, their regimental officers entertained themselves at a rowdy party in the governor's mansion. The time seemed right for a Federal surprise attack, yet Canby restrained his troops. At dawn, the Texans were astounded to find their foes right next to their camp, ready for battle. An artillery duel commenced immediately.

As the big guns thundered away at each other, a small Confederate supply train of seven wagons approached from the direction of Albuquerque. Itching for a fight, a company of Colorado cavalry charged like berserkers toward the wagon train and its small escort. After a brief but violent clash, the Colorado troopers emerged victorious, capturing all the wagons, one cannon, and twenty-two Texans. Meanwhile, Col. Green had ordered his men to take cover behind adobe walls and embankments as Union artillery shells continued to churn the sandy earth around them.

After a scouting report by Paddy Graydon, Canby sent troops along the brushy banks of the Rio Grande to prevent Confederate troops under Gen. Sibley and Col. Scurry, on the west bank, from crossing the river to reinforce Green's regiment on the east side. Nearly surrounded, Green ordered his troops to withdraw into the town of Peralta itself. Canby hesitated, not wishing to risk heavy casualties in house-to-house fighting. The cautious Federal commander only wanted his foes to continue their retreat from New Mexico Territory. Gritting their teeth and clutching their rifles tightly, the blue-coated troops reluctantly halted their advance. Increasingly strong winds whipped sand through their ranks as they took cover behind adobe walls and ditches, continuing to trade shots with their foes.

In the meantime, Scurry had successfully forced his way across the river to reinforce Green. Gen. Sibley himself, accompanied by a number of his staff officers, attempted to cross the river to get closer to the action. However, the general and his staff were driven off by heavy gunfire from Union pickets. Meanwhile, Union artillery shells continued to plague the Confederates. One exploded within the Texan field hospital. Another panicked their cattle herd, causing a stampede. One is reminded of the unsuccessful efforts of Paddy Graydon and his men at Valverde to stampede the Texan beef supply. Yet this "successful" stampede at Peralta headed in a very awkward direction: straight toward the Federal artillery. In a panic, the nervous Yanks frantically limbered up their big guns and hastily withdrew before being trampled. Soon, Texan cavalrymen recovered their herd and drove the confused steers back toward the Confederate lines.

By 2:00 P.M., a blinding sand storm had put an end to the gunfire. Canby withdrew his troops to their camp and the entire Texan army crossed the Rio Grande to the west bank,

The steers stampeded the Union guns.

discarding a great deal of their baggage to lighten the supply wagons for a speedy retreat. The Lone Star soldiers had just fought their last battle in the territory.

On the same day as the battle of Peralta, gunfire echoed through Picacho Pass north of Tucson. A detachment of Union troops from Fort Yuma, California, skirmished with Confederates led by Captain Sherod Hunter. Captain Hunter had been sent far west with only fifty-four men early in Sibley's New Mexico Campaign. The twenty-seven-year-old officer had first volunteered for Confederate service at Mesilla after Apaches had driven him from his farm in the Mimbres Valley. His boldness and daring in action soon impressed everyone, so Gen. Sibley had chosen him to command the small troop of cavalry to occupy Tucson and scout for any Union army movements from California. Indeed, hundreds of California volunteers and a company of the 3rd U.S. Artillery had gathered at Ft. Yuma under the command of Colonel James H. Carleton. Carleton made plans to march his force of 2,350 troops east to help crush Sibley's army. He sent out several small detachments in advance of his main force. These groups clashed with Hunter's men in obscure, nearly forgotten skirmishes that nevertheless have the historical distinction of being the westernmost armed engagements of the American Civil War.

First, Carleton sent Captain William McCleave with a small force of Federal cavalry to retake Tucson from Hunter and his men. However, the tables were soon turned by the clever young Confederate officer, who captured McCleave at the Pima Indian village near present-day Phoenix, Arizona. Next, Hunter's men busied themselves burning a large supply of Union cavalry hay and ran into another Federal detachment at a desert well site known as Stanwix Station. After a brief gunfight in which one California Yank was wounded, Hunter's Rebels rode off.

On April 15, Hunter's men had a much more serious shootout with a cavalry detachment under Lt. James Barrett in a pass dominated by a tall rock spire known as Picacho Peak. The desert combat north of Tucson, among the cacti and mesquite

Desert combat at Picacho Peak

trees, left three California troopers dead, including Lt. Barrett. The Yanks retreated from Picacho Pass, site of the westernmost deadly exchange of gunfire between Union and Confederate forces during the war.

Meanwhile, Col. Carleton's main force steadily marched toward Tucson. With his position untenable, Capt. Hunter finally evacuated the town on May 4 and rode east to the Rio Grande to notify Gen. Sibley of the approaching California column. During Hunter's retreat, he lost a total of four men to the marksmanship of hostile Apache warriors. Thus, Hunter's far-western military exploits, in what is today the state of Arizona, came to an end.

As Gen. Sibley continued his retreat on the west side of the Rio Grande, Gen. Canby kept up a relentless pursuit on the east side. On April 17, Canby even arrayed his force directly opposite Sibley's nervous troops, who avoided a confrontation, continuing their miserable march south. That night, Sibley called an officers' meeting. They all agreed that they could not risk another battle due to lack of ammunition. Of course, taking Ft. Craig from Kit Carson and his men was now entirely out of the question. At the urging of Col. Green, the Confederate general altered his route of retreat. Sibley chose to evade further encounters with his Federal foes by marching farther west of the Rio Grande and heading south through the untracked desert wilderness. Abandoning most of their remaining wagons, as well as their sick and wounded, the desperate Texans marched off into the night, away from the precious water of the Rio Grande, intending to circle around Ft. Craig and return to the river when they were far south of the post.

The long march became a grueling test of endurance and wilderness survival. Sibley's men began the nightmarish trek with a five-day ration of food and water. It was eight days before the advance units finally reached the Rio Grande once more. Water holes were few and far between. The desert was full of rough hills and ravines, making the transport of artillery next to impossible. Rope harnesses were fashioned to raise and

Col. James Carleton

lower the big gun barrels over countless terrain obstacles. Sick, exhausted, and dehydrated men were simply left by the wayside to feed the vultures. Discipline broke down and survival of the fittest became the primary rule. On April 25, Gen. Sibley finally reached the Rio Grande 40 miles south of Ft. Craig. The ragged, half-starved survivors of his desert death-march were strung out for 50 miles behind him. A year after the Texans' horrific march, a Union officer traveling over a portion of the same forbidding landscape found their route marked by discarded camp equipment, broken gun carriages, etc., with the sun-bleached skeletons of abandoned soldiers scattered amongst the debris.

Nearing the Texas border and refuge at Ft. Bliss, Sibley finally received the report from Capt. Sherod Hunter that Col. Carleton's California column was marching in his direction. There would be little time for his men to recuperate at Ft. Bliss. By May 4, Sibley had reached the post and had written the official report of his ill-fated New Mexico Campaign for the Confederate government. In it, he did not attempt to hide his own disillusionment: " . . . the Territory of New Mexico is not worth a quarter of the blood and treasure expended in its conquest." Days later, the bitter old general assembled the survivors of his army on Ft. Bliss's parade ground. There were still about 1,500 leather-tough Texans left. Over one thousand of their comrades were no longer present for roll call. Sibley thanked his troops for their devotion and self-sacrifice. They then prepared to march back to San Antonio; 700 miles more, across the plains of western Texas. All during the summer of 1862, groups of ragged, starving soldiers straggled into San Antonio's dusty streets. Most had already had their fill of war long before they reached home

Meanwhile, Col. Carleton's California volunteers continued their march as well. It was hard enough, even with proper supplies. Their progress through the desert met some resistance, although not from Confederates—it was from hostile Apache warriors. Several of Carleton's couriers were attacked by Chiricahua

Desert death-march

Apaches, members of a tribe led by the famous chief, Cochise. Then on July 15, a large advance column of supply wagons escorted by infantry, cavalry, and a battery of two howitzers, all under the command of Captain Thomas Roberts, was ambushed by the Chiricahuas at Apache Pass east of Tucson. The pass was the site of the only fresh water spring in the region, near an abandoned stage coach station flanked by steep, rocky hills from which the Apache snipers fired at Capt. Roberts' troops. At first the blue-coated soldiers retreated, but, utilizing their howitzers, they fought their way to the spring in order to get to water. The skirmishing continued for two days before Cochise's warriors finally withdrew, having suffered heavy casualties. Days later, when Col. Carleton arrived with more troops, he ordered the construction of a permanent post to guard the important spring for use by military and civilian travelers. The historic stronghold of stone and adobe buildings was named Fort Bowie and became one of the West's most notable frontier outposts.

Carleton and his men finally reached the Rio Grande, with his final detachment arriving in the middle of August. Gen. Canby gave Carleton permission to march into western Texas. The Californians reclaimed abandoned Ft. Bliss and Ft. Quitman for the Federal government. Finally, 200 miles into Texas, they rode into Ft. Davis and found one Confederate soldier. Long dead, his remains were pin-cushioned with arrows. There the Californians halted their advance. For the duration of the war, the far western reaches of Texas and all of New Mexico Territory remained in Federal hands. Col. Chivington marched his Pike's Peakers back to Colorado, where they received a rip-roaring heroes' welcome in Denver. Gen. Canby was reassigned to another position to the east and Carleton, promoted to brigadier general, took over command in New Mexico Territory. Kit Carson, an old Indian-fighting comrade of Carleton, retained his rank and joined the new Federal commander at his headquarters in Santa Fe.

In San Antonio, the survivors of Sibley's Brigade received a

The ambush at Apache Pass

sixty-day furlough to visit their families and recuperate. They would soon fight again. Led by Col. Tom Green and Col. William Scurry, they would participate in a dramatic action to retake Galveston, Texas, from Union invaders on New Year's Day, 1863. In time, Gen. Sibley himself would lead his Texans once more in an 1863 campaign in Louisiana. However, the gruff old general would make some military blunders that would result in his superior, Gen. Richard Taylor, demoting him to command merely the baggage wagon train.

Col. Tom Green, hero of Valverde, took over the command of the Texan brigade in southern Louisiana. The Lone Star soldiers in bayou country took with them the one prize they had saved from their grueling New Mexico adventure: the collection of six artillery pieces captured from McRae's Union battery at the Battle of Valverde. A specially trained artillery unit, made up primarily of members of the 5th Regiment, was equipped with the big guns. The Texans proudly called their outfit . . . the Valverde Battery.

CHAPTER 3

Ships, Sand, and Shells

Before the summer of 1862 was over, military action along Texas's Gulf coast heated up with a Union attempt to take Corpus Christi. An ambitious U.S. Navy lieutenant who had been blockading the coast, John W. Kittredge, boldly landed at Corpus Christi under a flag of truce. Backed up by his four well-armed gunboats, Kittredge demanded to be allowed to inspect Federal property within the city. The commander of local Confederate forces, Major Alfred M. Hobby, replied that no such property existed. Kittredge then gave Hobby a deadline of twenty-four hours to evacuate Corpus Christi before his ships opened fire. Another parley resulted in the truce being extended for another twenty-four hours.

Maj. Hobby did what he could to prepare his defenses within forty-eight hours. His militia force consisted of a handful of untrained volunteers and several artillery pieces left over from the Mexican War. Fortunately for the Texans, from that same old war, there were also sand-and-shell defensive embankments along the bay in a good position to challenge the Union gunboats which lay anchored only 400 yards out.

The dreaded deadline came at last—5:00 P.M. on August 15, yet the Federal guns remained silent. Maj. Hobby's men continued to work through the night on gun emplacements until 2:00 A.M. At dawn the Confederate defenders of Corpus Christi opened fire with six cannon from behind their sand defenses. Two of Kittredge's ships were struck by shells immediately as his sailors scrambled desperately to their battle stations. Soon the gunboats belched forth smoke and flame as they fired their salvos in reply. At first, the Yankee shells flew wild, missing their targets by far measure. As the cannon thunder rolled across the bay, Kittredge's men finally got the range of their targets, but their shells had little effect on the defenders' sandy walls. As Hobby's militiamen futilely sniped at the sailors with their muskets, one volunteer climbed atop their rampart and defiantly waved a homemade Confederate flag, stitched just the day before. After four hours of ship-to-shore action, Kittredge broke off the dramatic duel and withdrew his ships out of artillery range.

The next morning, Kittredge did not resume his attack but made plans for the following day. Meanwhile, the Texas militiamen busied themselves by retrieving any unexploded Union shells they could find in order to extract the gunpowder from them. Their powder supply was pitifully low. Approximately three hundred rounds had been fired at them by the U.S. Navy the day before. If they were going to survive another such attack, they needed to scrape together all the gunpowder they could find.

Early on the morning of August 18, Kittredge's ships sailed into gun range again. They opened fire once more as a landing party of about thirty sailors under Master's Mate Alfred Reynolds made it to shore in an attempt to flank the Texans. Reynolds' men were armed with muskets, pistols, cutlasses, and a howitzer which they struggled to haul along through the sand. To meet the Union threat on shore, Maj. Hobby sent a detachment of militiamen, including cavalry reserves under Capt. James A. Ware, to launch a counterattack. After a brief skirmish, the sailors were forced back to the water despite a heavy supporting fire of grapeshot from Kittredge's ships. After the failure of his landing party, Kittredge sailed off to repair his damaged gunboats and Corpus Christi remained in Confederate hands.

Kittredge's landing party

Although Kittredge had failed to capture the port, his threat to Corpus Christi was not over. He continued to blockade the region's coastline and captured a ship, the *Water Witch,* on August 23. In mid-September, the middle-aged former merchant marine officer went too far. He raided the southwest corner of Corpus Christi Bay and took several hostages at a community there called Flour Bluff. The Texans had finally had enough of his escapades. They set a trap for him. When Kittredge and his landing party came ashore again the very next day, they were soon surrounded by Capt. Ware's cavalry, who captured them without firing a shot. Thus ended Lt. Kittredge's naval operations at Corpus Christi.

Interestingly, not all the citizens of the bay area opposed the U.S. Navy, including the mayor of Corpus Christi himself. In fact, Union sympathizers were present in nearly all regions of Texas, although they were vastly outnumbered and frequently dealt with very harshly. When the Confederacy initiated conscription in the spring of 1862, many citizens objected so strongly that the situation nearly developed into a serious rebellion in Texas. Among the most adamant Union supporters opposed to the draft in the state were German immigrants located primarily in six counties along the west coast. Confederate authorities declared the counties in a state of rebellion and sent a detachment of cavalry to apprehend the ringleaders. In August a party of sixty-one German-Americans planning to flee to Mexico was overtaken by the Texas cavalrymen on the Nueces River. The troopers opened fire on the refugees and massacred thirty-four German men in cold blood, taking no prisoners.

Numerous other Union sympathizers could be found in the vicinity of Gainesville in north Texas. A few months after the Nueces River Massacre, over forty farmers and townsmen suspected of being Unionists were hanged in Gainesville. The search for "traitors" in Texas had become a terrifying witch hunt.

Other towns in Texas became the hosts of captive Union soldiers. Hempstead and Tyler both had prison camps located nearby. The compound near Tyler, Camp Ford, was the largest. It covered about 10 acres and was enclosed by a log stockade approximately 18 feet high. As many as 5,300 prisoners were confined at Camp Ford at one time or another during the war. The camp's population constantly fluctuated due to prisoner exchanges, parole, and numerous daring escapes. In contrast to such horrible prison camps as Andersonville, Camp Ford had a low death rate: only 206 graves were moved from the site after the war. Low mortality at the compound can mainly be attributed to an artesian spring located outside the western wall which provided fresh water that flowed in a creek through the camp. Survival inside Camp Ford was harsh, but there was enough food, shelter, and even occasional medical supplies to sustain human life.

In autumn, the U.S. Navy increased its activity along Texas's Gulf coast. On September 25, three Federal ships sailed into Sabine Pass, the outlet for the port of Beaumont, and opened fire on the Confederate battery there, known as Fort Sabine. It was located at the mouth of the Sabine River, which forms Texas's border with Louisiana. Unlike the garrison at Corpus Christi, the defenders of Ft. Sabine did not put up much resistance to the thunderous broadsides of the Union war ships. They spiked their artillery pieces, buried them, and swiftly evacuated the fort.

The next day the naval commander, Lieutenant Frederick Crocker, sent a large landing party ashore. They captured the nearby town of Sabine City, seized several blockade-running vessels, burned the local saw mill, and destroyed the railroad bridge over Taylor's Bayou, which led into Beaumont. However, Crocker's raiders had brought no occupation troops with them to hold what they had captured. Therefore the rampaging sailors simply reboarded their ships and sailed away to continue their blockade of the coastline. Crocker's destructive little raid made a lasting impression on local Confederate authorities, who made plans to improve defenses at Sabine Pass. The next time the Federals attempted to pull off an

Spiking and burying cannon

attack there, they would find stiffer resistance.

Also in September, Admiral David G. Farragut, commander of the West Gulf Blockading Squadron, outlined plans for the capture of Galveston, Texas. Farragut had captured New Orleans in April and now he wanted the important port of Galveston as well. Countless daring blockade runners continued to make it into the port despite the Federal patrols along the coast. Farragut ordered Commander William B. Renshaw to lead the Galveston expedition. On October 3, Comdr. Renshaw sailed into Galveston Bay with a fleet of four ships and sent an ultimatum to the Texans to surrender the city or endure a devastating bombardment of the port's defenses.

A "Mexican stand-off" ensued with each side holding its guns on the other for several days. Finally, the Confederates backed down and evacuated the city. On October 9, Renshaw took possession of Galveston. Interestingly, most of Galveston's citizens welcomed the U.S. Navy with open arms. However, once again troops necessary to occupy the captured seaport were not provided to the naval force. Renshaw nevertheless chose to hold his prize by utilizing his sailors as a daytime occupation force. Every night the seamen withdrew to the safety of their ships and returned to shore at daybreak. It was a risky operation, since Confederate forces were still within striking distance. Therefore Renshaw, as well as Farragut himself, continued to request that Federal troops be sent to hold Galveston for the Union. Finally, on Christmas Day, an advance detachment of the 42nd Massachusetts Infantry, 260 troops under the command of Colonel Isaac Burrell, landed at Galveston and barricaded themselves on the end of a brick wharf.

Meanwhile, the new Confederate commander in Texas, Major General John B. Magruder, had put Galveston at the top of his priority list. He immediately made plans to retake the important port with a joint land and sea operation. Magruder was a flamboyant man of action. A fifty-two-year-old professional soldier, but also an amateur stage actor, he was nicknamed "Prince John" for his thespian manners and lavish parties. Yet he had also made a name for himself as a fighter. A graduate of West Point, Magruder had served in the Seminole War and received three commendations for bravery in the Mexican War. When the Civil War began, he led Confederate troops in one of the first actions of the war, a skirmish in Virginia known as the Battle of Big Bethel on June 10, 1861, one month and eleven days before the Battle of Bull Run.

During the Peninsular Campaign in Virginia in the spring of 1862, Magruder had utterly confused General George McClellan and his Union army near Yorktown, causing him to far overestimate the size of the Confederate force he was wishing to attack. "Prince John" had cleverly marched the same small column of troops into the view of the Federals over and over again, as if endless reinforcements were arriving within his earthwork defenses. As a result, McClellan did not attack, but instead prepared for a massive siege, delaying his advance long

Maj. Gen. John Magruder

enough to seriously cripple the momentum of his campaign to take Richmond. However, later in the same campaign, Magruder had failed to impress his superior officers at the battles of Frayser's Farm and Malvern Hill, resulting in his transfer to the far West.

To retake Galveston Island, the imaginative Gen. Magruder assembled a makeshift naval force. He obtained two old steamboats, the *Bayou City* and the *Neptune,* and turned them into so-called cottonclads (rather than ironclads) by lining their decks with defensive walls of heavy compressed cotton bales. The dense bales could stop bullets and slow cannonballs. The cottonclads were also fitted with iron bowsprits, sharpened and barbed at their forward end to enable them to ram and hook onto enemy vessels. Magruder then manned his gunboats with 300 volunteers from Sibley's 5th and 7th Regiments under the command of the hero of Valverde, Col. Tom Green. Green's men jokingly referred to themselves as "Horse Marines" and boldly prepared to sail into Galveston Bay to take on the Union fleet.

Prince John also assembled a land force made up of more of Sibley's veterans of the New Mexico Campaign as well as local militiamen and some artillery, all under the command of William Scurry, who had been promoted to brigadier general since the Battle of Glorieta Pass. Scurry's land force, accompanied by Magruder himself, marched to a point opposite Galveston Island in preparation for their attack. They planned to cross over to the island on a two-mile-long railroad bridge which had been planked for troop movements by the earlier Confederate force at Galveston. Carelessly, the Union occupation force had left the planks intact and the bridge unguarded.

On New Year's Eve, the Confederate land force quietly crossed over to the island and deployed under cover of darkness as near to the barricaded wharf as they dared. At 5:00 A.M., with his usual dramatic flair, Gen. Magruder personally fired the first artillery round at the Union position on the wharf. Immediately, the early morning darkness was lit up by a spectacular fireworks display as both sides blasted away at each other with every gun they had. Manning one of the Confederate

Magruder's men made the night crossing on New Year's Eve.

artillery pieces was none other than John Baylor; shorn of his gubernatorial powers yet fiery as ever, he served as a cannoneer in the battle.

Comdr. Renshaw's fleet provided a devastating covering fire for Col. Burrell's Massachusetts troops, who fired volley after volley in defense of their fortified wharf. A charge in the early morning darkness was repulsed by the determined Union troops, supported by the big naval guns. The Confederate artillery positions on land became well-lit targets for the naval gunners every time a cannon barrel's muzzle flashed in the darkness as another round was fired. Thus the deadly shells from the Yankee ships landed in the midst of Confederate gun batteries on shore, forcing many a Rebel gunner to abandon his post.

Unable to advance in the heavy fusillade of shot and shell,

Magruder considered retreating. Then suddenly, in the early morning light, the two Confederate cottonclads steamed into view, heading for the nearest Union ship, the well-known *Harriet Lane*. This warship, a two-masted side-wheeler, had recently served as Admiral David Porter's flagship in the Union capture of New Orleans. The *Harriet Lane* cut loose with a roaring broadside to greet the approaching enemy vessels. One cottonclad, the *Neptune*, received a gaping hole below her waterline and slowly sank in the shallows with 150 Horse Marines scrambling for lifeboats. As the *Harriet Lane* maneuvered into a better position, she ran aground. Another Federal ship, the *Westfield*, had already run aground previously, leaving two Union vessels stranded. Suddenly the *Bayou City* surged forward and rammed the *Lane* as both ships fired point blank at each other, engulfed in swirling clouds of gunsmoke. Col. Tom Green's Texas riflemen poured a deadly hail of gunfire onto the deck of the *Lane*, killing the captain and mortally wounding her second-in-command. Then in true buccaneer style, the Texans clambered over the *Harriet Lane*'s gunwales, overwhelming her surviving crewmembers and capturing the famous warship. In a poignant moment reflecting the tragedy of broken families in the war, one Confederate officer, Major Alfred Lea, found his son, U.S. Navy Lieutenant Commander Edward Lea, lying mortally wounded on the ship's bloody deck.

Another Federal ship, the USS *Owasco*, approached the *Lane* and *Bayou City* and received a deadly fusillade of gunfire. After a brief attempt to return fire, the *Owasco* withdrew down the channel past another approaching warship, the *Clifton*. As the *Owasco* steamed out of harm's way past the fortified wharf, Col. Burrell signaled for her to stop and pick up his troops, who still desperately held their position despite the lack of covering fire from the navy. However, the *Owasco* failed to comply with Burrell's request. Meanwhile Commander Richard L. Law aboard the USS *Clifton* received the captain of the *Bayou City*, Henry Lubbock, who had boldly rowed out to his ship in a lifeboat flying a white flag. After a brief parley with the Confederate

In buccaneer style, the Texans boarded the Federal warship.

Major Lea found his mortally wounded son.

captain, Law agreed to a three-hour truce during which no ships would change position.

In the meantime, Col. Burrell, still stranded on the wharf, observed the white flags on the ships and requested a half-hour truce to ascertain his situation. Busy Capt. Lubbock of the *Bayou City* then rowed to Burrell's wharf and informed him that the three-hour naval truce did not pertain to his half-hour land truce and he better surrender before being overrun by overwhelming numbers of Texan soldiers. Thus the luckless Yankee colonel surrendered his Massachusetts troops, avoiding needless bloodshed.

Offshore, Comdr. Law had himself rowed out to the grounded USS *Westfield* to meet with the fleet commander on board the stranded warship just off an area known as Pelican Spit. Comdr. Renshaw informed Law that he intended to blow up the *Westfield* to prevent her from falling into enemy hands and then break the truce by escaping with the remainder of the Federal fleet. As Law returned to his own ship, Galveston Bay was rocked by the thunderous explosion of the *Westfield*. Tragically, she had exploded prematurely, after a fire had been set before all her crew had manned their lifeboats. Comdr. Renshaw and nearly twenty of his men were killed.

When Comdr. Law reboarded the *Clifton*, he observed that the Confederates, in violation of the truce, had moved the *Bayou City* and *Harriet Lane* near the docks while he had been conferring with Renshaw. He then signaled for all U.S. ships to leave the bay. As they steamed through the channel, Magruder's artillery on shore opened fire, but the parting shots failed to inflict any serious damage. At the mouth of the bay, Law learned of Renshaw's death and that he was now in command of the fleet. Four of his ships had been lost to the Texans: the *Harriet Lane*, the *Westfield*, and a couple of supply ships captured near the port. Considering a continuation of the Federal blockade to be fruitless, especially if the Texans utilized the formidable *Harriet Lane* as a Confederate warship, Law chose to sail his fleet away to New Orleans.

What followed was the biggest New Year's celebration Galveston has ever seen. Prince John's dramatic victory made front page headlines in newspapers across divided America. Sam Houston himself, despite his Unionist beliefs, wrote as a patriotic Texan to Magruder, congratulating him on reopening the important port. Admiral Farragut bitterly described the Union defeat at Galveston as having " . . . done more injury to the Navy than all the events of the war."

Farragut immediately ordered blockade ships back to Galveston. Only ten days after Magruder's victory, one U.S. warship and six gunboats arrived in the vicinity. One gunboat, the *Hatteras*,

Destruction of the Westfield

hailed a distant ship about 20 miles south of Galveston. The unidentified vessel slowly withdrew, followed by the *Hatteras*. Unknown to the gunboat's crew, they were simply being lured farther out to sea by a dangerous predator. The mystery ship was none other than the famous Confederate raider, *Alabama*. When her captain, Raphael Semmes, decided the gunboat was far enough from the rest of the Federal flotilla, he turned to attack. The surprised *Hatteras* crewmen worked their artillery as fast as they could but the *Alabama* had them outgunned. Roaring salvos from Capt. Semmes' heavily armed raider made short work of the Federal gunboat, which soon sank beneath the waves. The fearsome *Alabama* then sailed off in search of her usual prey, Union merchant vessels.

The Union navy experienced another setback later in the month at Sabine Pass, where Lt. Crocker's destructive little Federal raid had taken place the previous September. On January 21, two Confederate cottonclads, the *Josiah Bell* and the *Uncle Ben*, surprised and captured two small Union blockade ships near the pass, clearing the channel for Southern commerce. The Confederates had already strengthened the defenses of the nearby port of Beaumont by constructing a new fort with walls made of a mixture of oyster shells and mud. It was located seven miles above the mouth of the Naches River. In March they began work on another earthwork to replace old Ft. Sabine, abandoned during the previous year's raid. A team of thirty engineers and five hundred slaves constructed the new stronghold in a more defendable position that allowed a wide arc of artillery fire opposite the channel exits. The new little bastion was named Fort Griffin, but some still referred to it by the name of the old post, Ft. Sabine.

The cannon barrels which had been spiked and buried in September were recovered and repaired as more big guns were brought in to give Ft. Griffin plenty of firepower. It now had six in all: two 32-pounder smoothbores (guns capable of hurling 32-pound projectiles), two 32-pounder howitzers, and two 24-pounder smoothbores. The garrison consisted of forty-six Irish-

CSS Alabama

American volunteers of the Jeff Davis Guards, or "Davies" as they liked to call themselves. Officially, the Davies were a company of the 1st Texas Heavy Artillery Regiment that had already proved themselves worthy in battle at Galveston. The brawny Irishmen were dockworkers and railroad section hands recruited from the region of Galveston and Houston. Their commanding officer at Ft. Griffin, at the time of the upcoming Federal assault, was a twenty-five-year-old Houston saloon owner, First Lieutenant Richard W. "Dick" Dowling.

On September 5, 1863, a large Federal flotilla set forth from New Orleans bound for Sabine Pass. Eighteen transports were filled with 5,000 Union troops under Major General William B. Franklin, with ample rations and equipment for an invasion of Texas. Escorting the transports were four Federal gunboats commanded by none other than Lt. Frederick Crocker, the former whaling captain who had raided Sabine Pass the previous year. As the twenty-two naval vessels neared their destination, they split into two squadrons. One gunboat, the *Granite City*, was designated as a signal ship to precede the others to the channel entrance under the guise of a blockade ship. Under cover of darkness, she would signal the other Federal vessels on her seaboard side to the channel entrance and the entire invasion fleet would quietly slip into the channel in preparation for a surprise attack on Ft. Griffin at dawn on September 7. Unfortunately for the Federals, the nervous ship's master of the *Granite City* mistook a distant blockade ship on the horizon for the dreaded raider, *Alabama*. Not wishing to meet the same fate as the sunken gunboat, *Hatteras*, the *Granite City* swiftly fled the scene. What followed was an almost comical style of nautical confusion as both squadrons of ships, one under Lt. Crocker and one under Gen. Franklin, became disoriented and confused, hunting for the *Granite City*'s signal lights, as well as each other, in the darkness. By dawn they were still separated; the ships spent the entire day locating each other. By then they had been discovered by Confederates when some of Franklin's transports had moved up the channel in an effort to find the other vessels. It was nightfall before the entire Federal fleet was once again together. Crocker and Franklin knew the element of surprise was now lost but they planned to proceed with an attack at dawn before Confederate reinforcements could arrive at Ft. Griffin.

When news of the large Federal invasion fleet approaching Sabine Pass reached Gen. Magruder, he reluctantly issued orders for the tiny garrison at Ft. Griffin to blow up their defenses and withdraw. He could not get swift reinforcements to them and he did not expect a small handful of defenders to resist such overwhelming odds. But the Davies had earned a fighting reputation at Galveston and their pride would not permit them to leave Sabine Pass without making a stand. They and their young lieutenant chose to ignore the order to abandon Ft. Griffin. The brave Irish gunners had practiced faithfully with their artillery pieces and they knew the Yankee ships would make splendid targets.

At daybreak on September 8, Lt. Crocker steamed a short distance up the channel on his flagship, *Clifton,* and opened fire on Ft. Griffin to test the Confederate defenses. Staying beyond the accurate range of the fort's artillery, Lt. Crocker lobbed twenty-six explosive shells at the mud parapets with his big, long-range guns. Within the fort, Dowling and his Davies remained safely under cover in strong bomb-proof shelters roofed with heavy timbers and railroad iron. After an hour, the shelling ceased as the *Clifton* withdrew back across the channel's sandbar. Lt. Crocker then conferred with Gen. Franklin and his officers. Having met no resistance, the Union commanders confidently decided to enter Sabine Pass with all four gunboats and seven of their eighteen troop transports. The Federal plan of attack called for two gunboats, the *Sachem* and the *Arizona,* to spearhead the assault by moving up a far channel near the Louisiana shoreline, drawing Confederate fire. Then the *Clifton* would swiftly enter the channel near the fort, shelling the earthworks at close range. Behind the *Clifton,* the transports, defended by the guns of the *Granite City,* would land troops on the Texas shore to storm the fort.

At 3:40 P.M. the attack began when the two lead gunboats steamed ahead, firing their cannons as they drew closer to Ft. Griffin. The signal officer aboard the USS *Sachem* noticed their ship getting closer to what appeared to be target poles set in the mud of the Louisiana shore. Sure enough, the Davies of Ft. Griffin had been practicing their long-range marksmanship and when the gunboat drew abreast of the poles, the Irish gunners opened fire with deadly accuracy. One shell from the fort tore a hole through the *Sachem*'s hull and others plowed through the ship's wooden decks. Meanwhile, the USS *Arizona* was also drawing heavy fire as she struggled along behind the lead vessel. Near the head of the channel's oyster reef, the *Sachem* got stuck on a mudbank and in the next instant, a shell hit her main steampipe, spewing boiling water and clouds of steam over her splintered decks. Some of her crew panicked and jumped overboard.

During this impressive display of Confederate marksmanship, the USS *Clifton* began blazing away at Ft. Griffin once more as she steamed boldly up the channel. In the fort, Lt. Dowling immediately turned some of his guns on Crocker's flagship and soon one shot severed the *Clifton*'s tiller rope. The big gunboat went completely out of control, cutting through a marsh and running aground on the Texas shore. Crocker desperately attempted to keep all his starboard guns in action, firing on the fort, but several Confederate rounds struck the *Clifton*'s boiler, spraying his men with scalding water. Numerous screaming sailors abandoned their gun positions and jumped overboard. Dowling's men had now gotten the correct gun range of the *Clifton* as well as the *Sachem*, and the two U.S. Navy vessels became sitting ducks stuck in the mud. Thunderous explosions followed by showers of debris and wooden splinters now engulfed both ships. The *Arizona* continued to blast away at the gunsmoke-shrouded fort but she could barely defend herself, let alone come to the aid of her sister ships.

On board the *Clifton*, Crocker's men were falling fast from the incessant Confederate bombardment. The fiery explosions soon started a blaze that threatened to rage out of control. The former whaling captain who had been victorious at Sabine Pass the previous year now found himself utterly defeated. As the guns of Ft. Griffin thundered unmercifully, Crocker hoisted a white flag over the crippled USS *Clifton*. Immediately, another white flag went up over the *Sachem* as the *Arizona* sent out lifeboats to rescue as many of her sailors as possible. The *Arizona* then attempted to back out of the channel, getting stuck in the mud several times before she was finally able to break free and withdraw out of Confederate gun range.

Meanwhile, the *Granite City* and troop transports had watched all the devastating action from a distance. The only practical place to land Gen. Franklin's men was some firm ground that lay beyond the burning *Clifton*, and without that ship's protective covering fire, the transports would not move forward. Gen. Franklin ruled out the possibility of attempting to land his troops in the marshes, especially after a false report that a force of Confederate field artillery had been sighted approaching by land in the distance. Franklin concluded that there was simply no way to take Ft. Griffin under the present circumstances and the mission had failed. The signal flag for a withdrawal was hoisted and the Federal fleet headed back to sea, abandoning the *Clifton* and the *Sachem*. During the withdrawal, two transports became grounded on the channel's sand bar. To lighten their loads, they threw overboard 200,000 army rations and hundreds of mules and horses. The terrified animals were left to drown as the luckless Federal fleet sailed back to New Orleans, struggling through a fierce Gulf storm on the way.

As the smoke cleared in Ft. Griffin, Lt. Dowling took a head count. All forty-six of his Davies were unscathed! Sweaty and smeared with black gunpowder, the brawny Irishmen cheered ecstatically and searched for some whiskey to celebrate. Without losing a man, the handful of defenders had killed and wounded about 100 Federals, captured 350 (including Lt. Crocker), and taken possession of two Union warships and

Hundreds of mules and horses were driven overboard.

their thirteen artillery pieces. Most importantly, they had turned back a 5,000-man invasion force. Gen. Magruder reported the victory to Richmond, describing it as "the most extraordinary feat of the war." Dowling and his men became not only famous in Texas but heroes throughout the entire South. They received the thanks of President Davis and the Confederate Congress had a special medal struck to present to them. It was the only such medal presented to Confederate troops during the war. Another heroic person at Ft. Griffin during the battle was a widow from Sabine City who braved Federal artillery fire to bring food to the busy gunners. Kate Dorman was the owner and manager of the Catfish Hotel in town, which also served as a hospital for the wounded Union sailors after the battle.

For the duration of the war, the Federal government would not attempt to take Sabine Pass again. Yet a vengeful show of force was made in October when Federal ships shelled a Confederate stronghold known as Fort Esperanza on the coast south of Galveston at Matagorda Bay. Although the Texans temporarily retreated from their earthwork defenses during the punishing bombardment, the Federal flotilla had no troops to land, so the results were inconclusive. But a message had been sent to the Confederates: the Federal government was still not ready to give up on Texas. As a matter of fact, the Union high command, including President Lincoln himself, had decided that a Federal invasion of Texas must take place. Thus another Union invasion force, 6,000 strong, was quickly assembled at New Orleans. In command was politically ambitious Major General Nathaniel P. Banks, former governor of Massachusetts.

On November 2, after a sea-sick voyage through a Gulf storm, the Federal army landed unopposed near the Mexican border at Brazos Santiago, at the mouth of the Rio Grande, 24 miles from Brownsville. Gen. Banks' campaign plan was to occupy the mouth of the Rio Grande, close the Mexican border to Confederate commerce, then move up the coast and retake Galveston. Only a small force of Texas cavalry was present in the region to oppose Banks' army. The cavalry had little choice but to retreat. Before leaving Brownsville to the Federals, the troopers set fire to huge stores of cotton bales waiting to be traded across the border for European supplies. The fire spread, igniting caches of gunpowder. Fiery explosions rocked the community and showered flaming debris over a wide area. Much of the border town burned to the ground. Looting broke out and was only brought to an end when Banks' troops marched into town on November 6. The Federal occupation of Brownsville closed the lower Rio Grande to Confederate commerce, but the harm to Texas was minimal since the same trade was simply carried on farther up the river at Loredo and Eagle Pass. Nevertheless, trade was more difficult since cotton had to travel much farther by wagons before reaching the Mexican coast where European ships lay anchored offshore with badly needed rifles, medical supplies, and cloth.

Ten days after taking Brownsville, Banks moved up the Texas

coast, transporting a portion of his army by ships to secure strategic points. Confederate defenders on Mustang Island near Corpus Christi were shelled into submission and a Union garrison was left to occupy the island. Other successful landings were made farther north at Indianola and Port Lavaca. At Matagorda Bay, Ft. Esperanza was once again bombarded on November 27, as troops were put ashore to attack the fort from the rear. Sailors then hit the beach with howitzers to support the soldiers and the seashore stronghold fell soon after the dramatic display of Federal force.

As Gen. Magruder desperately prepared to defend Galveston with his limited manpower, a classic case of Federal bureaucratic bumbling took place which saved the important port from another attack. Although Banks' coastal campaign was off to a promising start (Pres. Lincoln himself had written the general to thank him for his "successful and valuable" operations), the Federal high command decided that a better plan to take Texas, as well as Louisiana, would be to proceed up the Red River rather than the Texas coast. In January 1864, General-in-Chief Henry W. Halleck, an egghead administrator sitting in Washington, succeeded in having most of Banks' army withdrawn from the Texas coast in preparation for what would become known as the Red River Campaign. The new plan was destined to lead to a disastrous Federal defeat in Louisiana. Although limited numbers of Union troops remained behind on Texas soil to precariously defend their small footholds along the coast and at Brownsville, the Lone Star State was no longer threatened by the presence of a large Federal invasion force. Thus the important port of Galveston was again saved for the South, this time not by force, but by the administrative incompetence of the Federal government.

CHAPTER 4

The Last Hurrah

By late 1863, violent, deadly raids by Navajo tribesmen had reached a bloody peak of ferocity in New Mexico Territory. Attempting to drive out Anglo and Hispanic settlers from their homeland, numerous Navajo warriors had launched an all-out effort to reclaim their territory. In response, Gen. Carleton, at his headquarters in Santa Fe, ordered Col. Kit Carson and nine companies of the 1st New Mexico Cavalry to establish a new fort inside Navajo country and wage a "vigorous war" against the tribe. The new post was named Fort Canby and from this base of operations, Carson waged a "scorched earth" campaign against his foes. The former mountain man destroyed everything of value to the Navajo he could find: lodges, crops, livestock, fruit trees, blankets, etc. Unable to replenish their supplies for the winter, Carson's foes faced starvation and freezing temperatures without adequate shelter.

The conquest of Native American homelands to create the nation we have today is indeed a dark chapter in United States history. Some historians have estimated that when Europeans first landed in the "New World," there was a total Indian population of about one million in North America alone. By the 1920s, their population had shrunk to only about 245,000. These figures reveal the horrible tragedy of a violent, deadly drama. Yet it is ludicrous to imagine millions of white settlers remaining crowded up along the east coast in an attempt to save the vast expanse of the entire continent for the exclusive use of only one million Native Americans. Even if larger population estimates are more accurate, such as a total of two or three million Indians, such numbers still make up a minuscule human population for the entire continent. By our standards today (when it is not uncommon for literally millions to live in one single city), North America would be considered nearly uninhabited with only a million people scattered like grains of sand across the vast landscape of the huge continent.

In the 20th century, public opinion has been greatly influenced by the way the film industry has portrayed the conquest of the West. Hollywood has attempted to recreate history in a typical "good guy versus bad guy" manner. Generally speaking, for fifty years in films, the Indians were the bad guys and the whites were the good guys. Then for the last twenty-five years, the Indians have been good and the whites have been bad. The truth is much more complicated. There have in fact been "good guys and bad guys" on both sides and each tribe's history has frequently presented a different sort of tragedy than another.

Even in the most idyllic situation imaginable, it would have still been impossible to prevent the inevitable clash of cultures that took place in the West. The truth is that civilization's "progress" has been grand but unmerciful. There is no way to stop its advance. Those who dare to stand in its way always face defeat.

On January 6, 1864, Col. Carson was prepared to strike a decisive death blow to the Navajo cause. On that day Carson led 389 New Mexico cavalry troopers out of Ft. Canby toward the Navajo stronghold: a narrow, 30-mile-long canyon with sheer red-rock walls, up to 1,500 feet high, known as Canyon de Chelly in what is today the state of Arizona. On January 12, Carson reached the canyon and in a brief desert skirmish killed eleven Navajo warriors. For the next three days, the cavalry relentlessly hunted their foes in the cold, stark landscape but never could force them into fighting a pitched battle. On the fourth day, sixty Navajos appeared at the cavalry camp begging

Col. Kit Carson at Canyon de Chelly

for mercy if they surrendered. Carson fed his starving prisoners and soon a steady stream of emaciated Navajo men, women, and children began surrendering to his command each day. Carson and his cavalry headed back to Ft. Canby trailed by a huge column of Navajo refugee-prisoners. Within three weeks, nearly 3,000 had surrendered. Within a few months, more than 8,000 people, nearly three-quarters of the once proud tribe, had become prisoners on the Bosque Redondo Reservation. Conditions were deplorable at the reservation where there were nowhere near enough government food rations for all the starving men, women, and children. The situation was so inhumane that even stern, cold-hearted Gen. Carleton put his own troops on half rations occasionally to provide extra food to the destitute Indian victims. Not until three years after the end of the Civil War would the Navajo be allowed to return to a portion of their homeland on a healthier reservation site.

By 1864, food had also become scarce in the entire state of Texas. Without men to work the fields, crops were sparse. Seeds to plant became more difficult to obtain. Landowners were urged to replace cotton with food crops but demand far exceeded supply and many Texans went hungry. To compound the problem, thousands of Southern refugees, fleeing invading Union armies in their own states, migrated to Texas. They and their slaves also needed food. Many of the refugees were Missourians fleeing the miserable guerrilla war in their state, such as John Shirley and his family. After Shirley's son was killed in a guerrilla skirmish, the family had left their home in Carthage, Missouri, and headed for Texas. They first settled in Grapevine and later moved to Scyene near Ft. Worth, where Shirley's teenage daughter, Myra Maybelle, would grow to womanhood. The family occasionally played host to other Missourians, including guerrillas who would head south when the leaves fell from Missouri trees each autumn, depriving the "bushwhackers" of their protective camouflage. Young Maybelle was profoundly affected by her brother's death at the hands of Federal authorities, the loss of her family's home in Missouri, and close association

Col. Kit Carson

with hardened, gun-toting guerrillas who sometimes visited the Shirleys' home in Texas. As a result, Maybelle chose a rebellious lifestyle and eventually gained notoriety later in life as Belle Starr, queen of the outlaws.

Even the exiled Confederate state government of Missouri had established its headquarters in Texas, where the town of Marshall became, in a sense, the secessionist state capital of Missouri. By and large, Missouri refugees conducted themselves as good Southern citizens in Texas. However, the Missouri guerrillas who wintered in Texas gained a nasty reputation as rowdy ruffians and were even blamed for acts of banditry by some Texans. "Bloody Bill" Anderson's guerrilla band went on drunken shooting sprees in the town of Sherman in January of 1864. Captain William C. Quantrill's command was also accused of similar unruly conduct. General Henry McCulloch considered the possibility of attempting to disarm and arrest Quantrill's men and stated in a letter to Gen. Magruder: "I regard them as but one shade better than highwaymen, and the community believe that they have committed all the robberies that have been committed about here for some time. . . . " Fortunately for the guerrillas, as well as the Texans, the Confederate governor of Missouri in Marshall wrote Quantrill on March 10, 1864, tactfully ordering him back to his own state: "General Smith is sending instructions partly at my suggestion to allow you to proceed within the enemy lines." Thus a violent showdown between Missouri guerrillas and Texas regulars was narrowly avoided in early 1864.

Meanwhile in southern Texas, Col. Rip Ford had mustered all the strength he could from local militia units and ragged, hungry volunteers. This group called themselves the Cavalry of the West. He intended to drive the small detachments of Federal troops from their strongholds along the Rio Grande. The sparse Union force was now under the command of a brave young major general named Francis J. Herron, who had earned the Congressional Medal of Honor for heroism at the Battle of Prairie Grove, Arkansas, in 1862. Yet bravery is of limited value when your troops are outnumbered and nearly abandoned by their government in a desolate region for which they have no desire to fight. Nevertheless, the Yankees skirmished with a detachment of Ford's irregular cavalry under Col. Santos Benavides outside of Laredo on April 15 before withdrawing farther downriver. Ford's hungry troopers pressed on, seizing several mud hut settlements along the river, but they found very few supplies to sustain themselves. The desperate Texas colonel resorted to drastic measures to save his command from starvation; he dispatched a raiding party into Mexico. The illegal Confederate raiders seized a large supply of Mexican cotton, which was sold to purchase essential supplies to revive Ford's rag-tag force of starving horsemen.

Suffering from recurring malaria, Rip Ford struggled to stay in his saddle as he led his motley cavalry farther downriver toward Brownsville. Bands of lean, haggard Texans and Mexicans, some of them border ruffians, joined his rough-cut little army as it rode in a dusty trail along the Rio Grande. Suddenly the blue-coats turned to briefly challenge the advancing column of Rebel troopers at Las Rucias Ranch on June 21. Gunsmoke mingled with clouds of desert dust under the sweltering summer sun as the Federal troops tested their pursuers' strength. Yet Col. Ford now had about a thousand men compared to the few hundred demoralized Yankee troops, and the Federals fell back, abandoning large quantities of desperately needed supplies at the ranch house.

With replenished strength, the sun-burnt Confederate column rode on to meet the remnants of the Union force at Fort Brown on the edge of Brownsville. After a hot little skirmish outside the frontier post on July 30, the Yanks set fire to their fort and abandoned Brownsville to the victorious Texas Rebels. No doubt it was a boisterous victory fiesta in Brownsville that night, celebrating the Texans' recapture of the Rio Grande valley. Tough old Rip Ford continued to pressure his Federal foes in the following months, finally forcing them to completely abandon the Texas mainland. The surviving Union troops entrenched themselves offshore on Brazos Island.

Meanwhile, the sad, unavoidable clash of cultures between Native Americans and white settlers continued to spill blood in the west. In the summer of 1864, Kiowas, Comanches, and Kiowa-Apaches raided the northern Santa Fe Trail with renewed ferocity. In September, Federal forces under Major General Samuel R. Curtis, commander of the Department of Kansas, pushed the hostile tribes south and the Indians migrated into the Panhandle region of Texas. In the Panhandle, the warring tribesmen raided settlements and hunted buffalo to build up their winter supplies of dried meat and blankets. Once again, Col. Kit Carson was assigned the task of dealing with the "hostiles." On November 12, Carson marched toward the Panhandle region with 335 California and New Mexico volunteers and 75 warriors of the Ute and Jicarilla Tribes. Carson was no Indian hater; he had numerous Native American friends and allies, many of whom served under his command in campaigns against hostile tribes. The old mountain man had infantry, cavalry, and two mountain howitzers with him on this expedition.

On the evening of November 24, Carson's scouts reported the discovery of a Kiowa-Apache village of about 170 lodges. The next morning, a frantic stampede of squaws and children took place as the blue-coats attacked. Numerous warriors, including the powerful Kiowa chief Little Mountain (who was visiting the village at the time of the attack), fiercely held back Carson's troops while their families evacuated the village. Finally, after a stubborn defense, the tribesmen themselves retreated down the Canadian River with a portion of the cavalry in close pursuit. The warriors' retreat continued until about a thousand Kiowa and Comanche men reinforced them from villages farther downriver. The stunned cavalry troopers dismounted and deployed as skirmishers in the tall grass around a cluster of ruins known as "Adobe Walls." The site featured the abandoned ruins of a trading post built by the fur trader William Bent a generation earlier.

Col. Carson soon arrived on the scene with the artillery and the balance of his force, except for a detachment of infantry which he had left to guard his supply wagons near the Indian village. Carson ordered his howitzers set up on a small hill and they immediately lobbed some shells toward their opponents, who retreated out of range of the big guns. The Indians had a special dread of cannon, which they called "guns that shoot twice" because of their ability to bring down more than one warrior with a single shot. However, about an hour later the Kiowas and Comanches attacked again with renewed strength as the Indian force swelled to perhaps as many as 3,000. Carson's small force desperately held back the encircling warriors of Little Mountain and other chiefs for several hours.

Finally Carson ordered a retreat from Adobe Walls back to the village. The Indians tried to prevent his escape by setting fires in the tall prairie grass, but the experienced Carson set fires of his own, strategically placed to give his troops safe passage across charred ground that their foes could not set ablaze again. At the village, more desperate fighting ensued but once again the howitzers were able to drive off the frenzied tribesmen. Carson then set fire to the village. The clever old scout-turned-colonel was then able to escape with his small force as his opponents busied themselves fighting the flames that were destroying their precious winter food and shelter supplies.

Only about twenty-five of Carson's men died from wounds received in the savage day-long struggle. Carson estimated he had killed and wounded at least sixty Kiowas and Comanches. The amazing fact is that the Federal force was not completely wiped out. If it weren't for the howitzers and Carson's own cunning ability as a commander, the action would probably be remembered as the Adobe Walls Massacre. Twelve years later another U.S. Army officer faced similar odds along the Little Bighorn River in Montana and did not fare so well.

Although the first Battle of Adobe Walls (the second would be fought ten years later in 1874) was the most dramatic Indian fight in Texas during the Civil War years, it was certainly not the only one. Another large clash between Native Americans

Charred ground at Adobe Walls

and their Anglo American opponents in Texas during those hard years took place at Dove Creek, about 16 miles south of present-day San Angelo. It was fought in the bitter cold on January 8, 1865, between warriors of the Kickapoo Tribe and Texas militiamen and Confederate cavalry troopers, assisted by Tonk Indian scouts. Tragically, it was entirely unnecessary. Unknown to the Texans, the large number of Native Americans moving through the state were simply on their way to Mexico from Kansas. Kansan and Mexican authorities had given them permission for the move but had failed to notify Texan authorities, who panicked at what they believed to be a major foray of "illegal" Indian invaders.

About 1,500 Kickapoo people were trailed by twenty Texas militia scouts, who ascertained the identity of the tribe by opening a fresh grave on their trail. Some of the men opposed the grave-pillaging that took place in which various beads, trinkets, moccasins, and articles of clothing were removed from a richly adorned Kickapoo woman's corpse. However, the souvenir hunters merely laughed at their superstitious comrades who warned against "bad medicine." A few days later, in the Battle of Dove Creek, each man who had possession of one of these burial souvenirs was killed in action.

On the morning of January 8, over five hundred Texans were poised to assault the Kickapoo camp. The attacking force consisted of about four hundred civilian militiamen under Captain Totten, 110 Confederate cavalry troopers under Captain Henry Fossett, and a number of Tonk tribesmen allied with the Texans. In the initial assault, Fossett's troopers and the Tonk tribesmen, along with a few militiamen, launched a mounted charge on the Kickapoos' horse herd, capturing nearly a thousand Indian ponies near the camp. Meanwhile, the main Texan assault was made in a dismounted fashion since most of their horses were exhausted after the long ride to the battle site. The hardy Texans waded through ice-cold Dove Creek, in places waist deep, to reach the Kickapoo camp. Capt. Totten's militiamen fought desperately for an hour at the camp and then were forced to retreat before the superior firepower of the warriors. Surprisingly, the Kickapoos were better armed than the Texans! Many Kickapoos had served in the 2nd Indian Home Guard, a Union regiment that fought in actions in Missouri and Indian Territory (present-day Oklahoma). They had government-issue, long-range, military rifles while the Texans had mainly shotguns and civilian rifles. The Kickapoo chief, No-Ko-Wat, was an experienced warrior who could understand the commands shouted by his Texan foes. When he heard the order to retreat shouted from the Texan line, he led his braves forward in a howling charge, resulting in desperate hand-to-hand combat. A number of Texans lost their lives in the savage fighting which ensued.

For five hours the battle raged back and forth along Dove Creek. Sporadic skirmishing continued until nightfall with the Kickapoos recapturing most of their horse herd before retiring back to their camp. The shot-up Texan force retreated, taking their dead and wounded with them. Texan losses totaled twenty-three killed outright with sixty seriously wounded, some of whom died later. Sixty or seventy Texan horses had also been killed. The Kickapoos left that night, abandoning twenty-three dead and much of their camp equipage on the frozen battlefield in their haste to escape the senseless violence. The hard feelings from this tragic encounter no doubt led to the rash of devastating Kickapoo raids into southern Texas from Mexico during the years following the Civil War.

Just as the Texans rode into battle against the Kickapoos without considering the consequences, so the Lone Star State had charged headlong into the Civil War on the side of the Confederacy. Texas contributed nearly 90,000 men to the Confederate Army out of a total population of slightly over 600,000. The Texas soldiers made up forty-five regiments and twelve battalions of cavalry, twenty-three regiments and four battalions of infantry, and one regiment of heavy artillery and thirty batteries of light (field) artillery.

Texan units could be found in every theater of the war. The most renowned was the Texas Brigade, which fought in the

Eastern Theater in General Robert E. Lee's Army of Northern Virginia. The brigade's commander, General John B. Hood, gained fame as one of the toughest (although not tactically brilliant) fighting commanders of the Confederacy. Hood's Texas Brigade first earned glory at the Battle of Gaines' Mill on June 27, 1862, during the Seven Days Battles when Gen. Lee pushed General George B. McClellan out of Virginia and saved Richmond from being captured early in the war. At Gaines' Mill, the Texans overran a heavily entrenched Federal position, securing victory for Lee in the hard-fought battle. Their bravery cost the brigade 570 killed and wounded.

The Texas Brigade saw continuous action throughout the war, fighting in such famous battles as 2nd Bull Run, Antietam, Gettysburg, Chickamauga, and the Wilderness. Almost always outnumbered, the brigade relied on its own bravery and ferocity to survive. Gen. Hood favored slug-it-out tactics, especially headlong charges against enemy positions. At the Battle of Antietam, Maryland, on September 17, 1862, the Texas Brigade lost 560 of the 854 troops it had present. On the second day of the epic Battle of Gettysburg, Pennsylvania, on July 2, 1863, the 4th and 5th Regiments of the Texas Brigade launched repeated assaults on Union troops desperately holding the Federal line on Little Round Top. The savage fighting on this portion of the field would gain legendary status. At Chickamauga, Georgia, September 19-20, 1863, two regiments (normally about a thousand men per regiment) emerged from the furious carnage with less than a hundred men each and one company had only one survivor. At the end of the war, only 557 men of the 4,480 who served in the Texas Brigade were living.

At the siege of Vicksburg, Mississippi, Texas troops also earned a fighting reputation. On May 22, 1863, five Federal regiments charged the 2nd Texas Infantry Regiment under Colonel Ashbel Smith. Outnumbered about five to one, the Texans threw back the repeated assaults and stubbornly held their position. The same day, Waul's Texas Legion, commanded by Colonel Thomas N. Waul, dramatically overwhelmed a well-fortified Union position that had previously withstood numerous assaults.

One of the most respected units fighting for the Confederacy was Terry's Texas Rangers. Led by Colonel B. Franklin Terry, the Rangers were widely celebrated as some of the bravest fighting men in the war and proved it at the monumental Battle of Shiloh, Tennessee, on April 6-7, 1862. By the end of the war, Terry's Texas Rangers had lost two-thirds of their men as well as Col. Terry himself.

Texas enthusiasm could sometimes backfire, resulting in defeat rather than victory. On July 17, 1863, at the Battle of Honey Springs in Indian Territory, men of the 29th Texas Cavalry (fighting on foot) took advantage of a lull in the enemy gunfire and advanced, hoping to secure a Confederate victory. Unknown to the dauntless Texans, troops of the 1st Kansas Colored Infantry waited in the tall prairie grass for them, loaded and ready to fire. The devastating Union volleys, fired point-blank at the line of advancing Texans, decimated their regiment. Their resulting retreat spread to the rest of the Confederate army and the entire Southern battle line fell apart like a row of falling dominoes; a cruel fate for a brave effort.

Meanwhile, back in Texas, fighting had nearly ceased between the Federal government and Confederate forces after Col. Rip Ford had pushed the Yanks off the mainland onto Brazos Island in the summer of 1864. However, by the spring of 1865, scattered skirmishing was again taking place as Federal patrols were occasionally sent to scout the mainland from their island stronghold, which had received hundreds of reinforcements. By that time, desertion had become rampant in the Confederate forces, drastically reducing the number of men who remained in active military service in Texas. About three thousand were around Galveston and Houston while the rest were in small, scattered garrisons at Corpus Christi, Hempstead, Sabine Pass, Marshall, Austin, San Antonio, and Brownsville. Governor Pendleton Murrah promised deserters a full pardon if they would return to their units. However, the military strength of Texas continued to dissolve as troop morale reached new lows with news of Confederate defeats back East.

News of Gen. Lee's surrender in April was slow reaching Texas garrisons. Rip Ford and his men in the Brownsville region had not yet heard the news when a sizable Federal force was ordered out from their Brazos Island camp in May. The commander of the Brazos camp, Colonel Theodore Barrett, ordered 250 men of the 62nd U.S. Colored Infantry and 50 troopers of the dismounted 2nd Texas (Federal) Cavalry to gather up stray bands of Confederates and occupy Brownsville. The African-American troops, assisted by the white cavalrymen, were under the command of Lieutenant Colonel David Branson, who expected no serious resistance, assuming that the demoralized Texans had been informed the war was basically over.

At 8:30 A.M. on May 12, Lt. Col. Branson and his men arrived at Palmito Ranch along the Rio Grande northeast of Brownsville. There they found a Confederate cavalry camp of about 150 men under Captain W. N. Robinson. Branson was cautious enough to deploy his men for battle just in case there was trouble, and sure enough, there was. Capt. Robinson did not intend to surrender and a sharp skirmish between the two forces lasted throughout the morning. Around noon, the outnumbered Texans finally withdrew, leaving the Federals in possession of the ranch, three prisoners, a small cattle herd, and the Confederates' supply of food rations. Branson burned the Texan camp, then posted his men on a nearby hill. Surprisingly, Capt. Robinson and his bold Rebel troopers, fighting mad about losing their food supply, counterattacked late in the afternoon. Lt. Col. Branson assumed that the Texans had been reinforced and chose to pull back farther east to White's Ranch. In reality, the Texans had not yet received help but reinforcements were indeed being assembled by Col. Rip Ford at Brownsville, only 12 miles away. Meanwhile Branson sent a courier to Brazos Island requesting additional troops due to the resistance he had met.

Early the next morning, Col. Barrett arrived at White's

Ranch with 200 troops of the 34th Indiana Infantry, "the Morton Rifles." Taking personal command of the approximately 500 Federal troops, Barrett marched toward Palmito Ranch. Once again, Capt. Robinson and his troopers were forced to abandon the field to the Yanks. Col. Barrett then ordered the ranch buildings burned. Word of the renewed combat reached Col. Ford's column of Confederate reinforcements in the afternoon as they advanced on the Brownsville Road. Ford had hastily assembled 200 cavalrymen and a battery of four artillery pieces. Interestingly, a number of gunners manning Ford's artillery were Frenchmen from across the Mexican border who had volunteered to help. At this time in Mexico's turbulent history, the puppet Emperor Maximilian was in power with a French army of Napoleon III, ruler of France. The French were somewhat sympathetic to the Confederate Texans and likewise unfriendly to U.S. forces.

By a forced march, Col. Ford and the Texan reinforcements rode onto the San Martin Ranch at 3:00 P.M. to the sound of gunfire. There, Capt. Robinson and his troopers were making a stand after being pushed west of Palmito Ranch. Robinson's men ceased fire long enough to cheer Ford as he galloped onto the field. Cheers of "Hurrah for old Rip!" rang out as the old Texas Ranger waved his hat in the air, shouting words of encouragement to his troops. It was the South's last hurrah. Historians consider this action in Texas on May 12-13, 1865, along the Rio Grande, to be the last battle of the American Civil War.

"Old Rip" quickly deployed his artillery and sent a flanking force of cavalry forward, pushing back the Federals, who had no artillery support. The Yanks put up a dusty, fighting retreat for 8 miles to the east, past Palmito Ranch and White's Ranch. In the middle of the blazing action, Ford's artillerymen and cavalry troopers received some unexpected reinforcements from south of the Rio Grande. A force of Imperial (French) Mexican Cavalry arrived on the scene and deployed for battle on the south side of the river. According to Col. Barrett's official

French and Confederate cavalry soldiers

report of the action, his men were fired upon from across the river by the French cavalry detachment.

The Union retreat was exhausting for the hard-pressed infantrymen, and the color bearers of the 34th Indiana were unable to keep up with the main force. Thus the Morton Rifles lost both their regimental flag as well as the national colors during their hasty retreat. With the Federals nearly routed, more Confederate troops arrived on the field under Ford's commanding officer, Brigadier General James E. Slaughter. The outgunned Yanks skedaddled back to Brazos Island. The Confederates had won the last battle of the War Between the States.

At twilight the action fizzled out east of White's Ranch as the last exchange of gunfire took place. In Col. Barrett's report of the battle, he describes what some consider to be the last shots of the war: "The last volley of the war, it is believed, was fired by the 62nd Colored Infantry, about sunset of the 13th of May 1865, between White's Ranch and the Boca Chica, Texas." Exact casualties are unknown but estimates indicate that about fifty or sixty total were killed and wounded with losses about even on both sides.

The 113 Federals taken prisoner by Ford's men at the Battle of Palmito Ranch informed the Texans of Lee's surrender back East. Several days later, Union officers rode into Brownsville to confer with Gen. Slaughter and Col. Ford, resulting in Confederate forces in the region being disbanded. Yet for a brief time, some Southern leaders urged continued resistance.

On May 13, the same day gunfire echoed along the Rio Grande at Palmito Ranch, a conference of Confederate Trans-Mississippi governors and military officers convened in Marshall, Texas, to consider an offer to surrender on the same terms Lee had accepted from Grant. Yet the mood of the conference was defiant and it failed to produce a solution at all. As a matter of fact, one still rebellious officer, Major General Joseph O. Shelby of Missouri, urged continued resistance and proposed the possibility of crossing the Mexican border and establishing a Confederate colony. A number of officers agreed with the fiery Shelby, who had the reputation of being one of the South's finest cavalry leaders. However, by the end of May, the commander of the Trans-Mississippi Department, General Edmund Kirby Smith, had come to realize the futility of further resistance. His chief of staff, Lieutenant General Simon B. Buckner, surrendered on paper all Confederate forces west of the Mississippi—subject to the approval of Gen. Smith—in New Orleans on May 26, 1865, to Gen. Edward Canby, victor of the New Mexico Campaign. The articles of agreement were dispatched by special steamer to Galveston. There on June 2, aboard the U.S. warship *Fort Jackson* anchored in the harbor, Gen. Smith signed the terms of capitulation. Confederate military personnel were to be paroled to return to their homes and all Confederate property was to be surrendered to Federal authorities.

The American Civil War, or War Between the States, was finally at an end. Yet the last great drama of the conflict was yet to be played out. Gen. J. O. (Jo) Shelby chose to go through with his plan to march his cavalry volunteers across Texas into

Maj. Gen. Jo Shelby

Mexico and establish a Confederate colony south of the border. About a thousand Missouri and Arkansas troopers from his old "Iron Brigade" rode south, trailed by a battery of artillery and a long train of supply wagons. A number of other general officers and political leaders, including Gen. John Magruder, Gen. E. Kirby Smith, and the Confederate governors of Texas, Missouri, and Louisiana, also joined the exodus. Hoping to win favor and land in Mexico by serving in Emperor Maximilian's army, Gen. Shelby and his men rode toward the Rio Grande with their Confederate battle flag still flying proudly at the front of their column.

While crossing Texas, Shelby and his men were called upon to restore order in a number of towns where civil authority had broken down with the collapse of the state's Confederate government. The most serious incident took place in Austin. The state capitol building housed the state treasury as well as a sub-treasury department of the Confederate government. A total of $300,000 in gold and silver was stored in the building, guarded by only a handful of soldiers. A large force of bandits, led by a notorious bushwhacker known as Captain Rabb, attempted to raid the capitol and seize the treasure. Rabb planned his raid when Shelby's force was camped near Austin with the hope that Shelby and his men would be blamed for the robbery. Little did he know that Shelby's troopers would be his downfall.

Rabb's bandits filtered into town one rainy night and took their places at various locations, waiting for the designated time of attack. When the time came, they mounted their horses and converged, riding hard for the capitol building. They gunned down the unfortunate guards and began to hammer away at the iron doors of the massive treasury safes. Church bells in town began to ring, sounding the distress signal for Austin's company of civilian home-guards to assemble at the town armory. A courier was dispatched to Shelby's camp with a request for aid to save the treasury. Soon the blare of a cavalry bugle could be heard as a column of Shelby's troopers galloped into the town square, where the mayor urged them to proceed with all haste to the state house.

By the time Shelby's rain-soaked men reached the building, the raiders had succeeded in battering down the treasury doors and were in the process of looting the ample supply of gold and silver coins. There was a flurry of gunfire as the Confederate troopers made short work of Rabb's guards stationed outside the building. Soon the guns sounded again, louder and more numerous, as some of Rabb's band rushed from the building to meet their adversaries. The bandits were driven back inside as Shelby's men followed close behind, sweeping through the doors and blasting away with their carbines and pistols. The thieves were no match for the veteran cavalry troopers and were mercilessly gunned down in the midst of the scattered gold and silver coins of the treasury.

Rabb and a few others escaped, leaving a mile-long trail of shining coins lying in the muddy streets of Austin. But nearly all the treasury had been saved. The grateful governor of Texas urged Gen. Shelby to take the Confederate government's portion and use it to pay his own unpaid soldiers, whom the governor recognized as elements of the last surviving military force of the Confederacy. However, the chivalrous Shelby refused the generous offer and soon marched his command onward to San Antonio.

Before reaching San Antonio, Shelby's command had a wild night skirmish with a large force of bandits attempting to steal the cavalry's horses. A total of thirty-nine dead rustlers lay motionless in the dust as a result of their brash attempt to steal from the vigilant, battle-hardened force of Confederate veterans. Upon reaching San Antonio, Shelby found it necessary to put the town under martial law because the lawless elements had taken over the community, terrorizing honest citizens. Thieves and murderers were dealt with harshly, some being literally pushed into the San Antonio River while attempting to escape justice. As Shelby's adjutant, Major John Edwards wrote, "Some men are born to be shot, some to be hung, and some to be drowned."

As Shelby's column drew closer to Eagle Pass, where he planned

The treasury thieves were no match for Shelby's troopers.

to cross the Rio Grande, a Federal cavalry force of 3,000 men and six artillery pieces drew close in pursuit. At one point in time, the Federals deployed for battle within sight of the Confederates, who also prepared for action, but at the last moment the U.S. Cavalry withdrew. They were content to let Shelby's men ride on toward the border, thus avoiding needless bloodshed after they had performed the last hostile military maneuvers of the war.

At last Gen. Shelby's force reached Eagle Pass. It was there, at that dusty Texas border town, that the Missouri and Arkansas cavalry troopers performed a simple yet profound act signaling the end of the Confederate Cause. On July 4, 1865, the tattered, bullet-riddled battle flag of Shelby's command was lowered into a watery grave in the Rio Grande. In a solemn ceremony at a wide and fairly deep portion of the river known as Rio Bravo del Norte, five colonels held their beloved banner up for their men to view one last time. The hardened soldiers of the South broke down and wept like children as their hearts broke with grief. All they had fought and bled for; the cause for which they had sacrificed everything . . . was dead. The colonels weighted the beloved cloth symbol and waded far out into the river, then gently lowered the banner into the water. It was the last battle flag to fly over an armed, defiant Confederate force. Undefeated in spirit, Shelby's troopers then crossed over into old Mexico flying only a guidon in place of their never-surrendered Southern banner. The Civil War in Texas, and in the rest of the reunited nation, was over.

Due to the bravery of its defenders and its geographical location, the Lone Star State was never successfully invaded during the war. Therefore its citizens were spared the accompanying hardships that numerous other Southern states suffered. Also, trade with Mexico helped keep the Texas economy solvent. Thus another great problem that most other Southern states experienced, a destroyed economy, was avoided by Texas. However, massive food shortages and the loss of thousands of its best young men had been hard indeed. Bloodshed, destruction, death, and defeat had been the wages of fighting for the

The symbol of their lost cause was lowered into a watery grave.

Confederacy. The man who had tried to warn his fellow Texans against it all, Sam Houston, had died on July 26, 1863, a broken-hearted old patriot, believing his entire life had been merely a failure in the end. Yet the great Texas legacy of outstanding military feats of courage and daring from 1861 to 1865 cannot be denied nor forgotten. It is a brave, adventurous, and inspiring chapter in the terrible yet thrilling story of America's Civil War.

Refighting the War

The stern, threatening beat of military drums rolled across the dusty fields near Grandbury, Texas. Long lines of men in blue and gray marched grimly toward each other in preparation for battle. The date was September 21, 1996. For the education and entertainment of the general public, history was being brought back to life with a simulated Civil War scene. In Texas, New Mexico, Oklahoma, Kansas, Missouri, Arkansas, and Louisiana, the war west of the Mississippi is portrayed time and time again. In states from Virginia to California, spectacular battles from the great War Between the States are reenacted throughout the year.

The rough old days of the American Civil War are long gone . . . thank goodness. No one in their right mind would wish to return to such a hard and cruel time. Yet if the reader enjoys tales of adventure as much as I do, he or she can understand how a person could become fascinated with such a bold and dangerous era in our nation's history. Those who have developed such a fascination may choose from a massive variety of books dealing with the subject of Civil War history. A good number of high quality video tapes on the subject have also become easily available. Also, numerous fine battlefield parks exist for the education and pleasure of those who are curious enough to pay a visit. But of all the outlets for the passions of a

Photo by Rhonda Cottrell

Civil War hobbyist, the most unique is the extraordinary activity known as reenactment. Although nothing will ever replace books as a source of knowledge, the physical experiences of participating in mock battles, marches, drills, and encampments create sensations that no book could ever achieve. Many of these sensations bring the participant closer to the far-distant past of the Civil War Era:

Damp, itchy, wool uniforms on a hot summer day. Sore feet rubbing against the hard, wooden-pegged soles of dusty "brogans." The noisy clanking of a tin cup and canteen dangling from cumbersome gear. A nine-pound rifled musket that seems to grow heavier with every mile of march. The rattle of musketry in the distance as your column moves forward at the "double-quick" to engage the enemy. The burning smell of sulfurous gunsmoke swirling around you like angry storm clouds. The bitter taste of gunpowder as you tear open a paper cartridge with your teeth.

One can attempt to merely imagine such sensations, but imagination cannot equal physical experience. Any brief moment of stark realism that is generated during a reenactment event is a rare window to the past and is a worthwhile reward for the hard, meticulous work that goes into the reconstruction of an accurate historical scene.

However, there are times when realism goes too far: real casualties occur occasionally no matter how many precautions are taken by a safety-conscious reenactment organization. I recall the day down in Eureka Springs, Arkansas, in 1984 when the unit I was serving with faced a long line of enemy infantry and a slick pool of blood filled my hand, causing my rifle to slip from my grip. A fall I had taken earlier among some sharp rocks had left my hand sliced wide open. The dirty bandanna I used to bind the gash until the end of the battle probably had something to do with the purple and yellow streak that began to climb up my arm days after the wound had been sewn shut. I have often thought of how a simple shot in the doctor's office in 1984 took care of the infection that probably would have

Photo by Steve Cottrell

resulted in an arm amputation in 1864. Hence I have a greater appreciation for living in modern times.

Accidents such as my fall are unavoidable, yet sometimes lack of caution results in more serious incidents. I remember the rain-soaked reenactment of the Battle of Pilot Knob, Missouri, in 1983 when I was serving in a Confederate cavalry unit. A line of Union infantrymen leveled their rifles in our direction and, in the customary cavalry fashion, I leaned forward in the saddle with my head tucked low in anticipation of their volley. They fired and to my astonishment, a projectile grazed me just above my left boot and slammed into the leg of a trooper behind me. For an instant I was dumbfounded with the notion that we had actually been fired upon! A hasty investigation revealed that the projectile was a wooden plug which is commonly used to seal the muzzle of a military musket to protect the inner barrel, especially during rainy weather. The plug was turned over to our enraged captain, who immediately let his feelings be known to the offenders and those in charge of the event.

A cavalryman has a big problem other reenactors don't have: a horse. I recall the dilemmas I experienced during my two years in a cavalry unit, including the problem of just trying to maintain my balance in the saddle during chaotic battle simulations. After one spectacular fall, a wide-eyed spectator came up to me when the "battle" was over and asked how I could perform such amazing stunts. Rather than explain how it was all just an accident, it seemed easier to reply, "It takes a lot of practice." I admit that some of my equestrian difficulties were nobody's fault but my own. I remember the time I fired my revolver directly over my mount's head. The gunblast burnt the tip of the poor creature's right ear. He took swift vengeance, treating me to a rodeo-style bronco ride I'll never forget. When firing a revolver from horseback, it should be done from the side. Everyone makes mistakes, but blunders involving gunfire (even blank loads) can be risky.

The most incredibly dangerous blunder I ever witnessed

Photo by Bob Tommey

Photo by Bob Tommey

occurred in a tactical war game near Roscoe, Missouri in 1984. The "tactical" took place in the early morning hours prior to public visitation (as they should) and featured specific objectives as well as judges to perform scoring duties. I was with a Union infantry company (I have marched with both sides and continue to do so). We had nearly reached our final objective when our scouts reported that a large force of Confederates was just down the road on which we were marching. Our captain marched us off the road and we took to the woods, silently nearing the enemy position. We had a very poor view of their movements and activities as we crouched low in the dense brush. We could see a small wooden structure in the road, resembling a miniature cabin. A few Rebel commands were audible: they were preparing to fire an artillery piece. The big

Photo by Steve Cottrell

gun sounded extra loud and the subsequent fireball explosion which engulfed the wooden shack no more than 50 yards from our position made my mouth drop open in amazement. Only about fifteen minutes earlier we had been marching on that road, heading in the direction of the violent inferno we just witnessed.

In retrospect, after this first barrage, we probably should have started yelling, "Cease fire!" However, we remained frozen in an astonished trance as preparations were made for a second salvo. The cannon roared again and another pillar of fire erupted in the same general area near our concealed unit. We then listened to a rousing series of Rebel yells and a flurry of commands as the enemy infantry marched off down the road. Our scouts reported that the artillery crew was preparing to haul off their cannon on a mule-drawn gun limber. As soon as the Confederate infantry was out of sight, our 1st sergeant, Bill Fannin, led us in a glorious charge upon the limbered gun and its surprised crew who had no choice but to surrender. We reached our final objective and won the tactical . . . without any casualties.

Of course an investigation of the live fire incident immediately took place once both sides were back in camp. Our Confederate brothers at first claimed it was our own fault for being in the wrong place at the wrong time. They said we began our maneuvers before the designated starting time and that they had scheduled their live fire demonstration safely one half-hour before the tactical was to begin. Our officers pointed out that the official schedule indicated we had begun our maneuvers at the proper time and if the members of the Confederate organization wanted to continue to have Union troops present at their events, they had better put safety first. It was finally agreed that live fire anywhere but on a designated firing range was dangerous and henceforth strictly forbidden; especially hot canister fired into wooden shacks containing jugs full of gasoline. As far as I know, this was the last recorded instance of troops wearing Union blue endangered by live fire from troops in Confederate gray. Surely Roscoe, Missouri, could not take the place of Palmito Ranch, Texas! By the way, every man in our Union infantry unit, Holmes' Brigade, that was present for duty that morning was later awarded a specially engraved medal for bravery "under fire."

In November of 1985 our unit got to participate in an extraordinary occurrence that will always stand out in my mind as being the closest thing to real Civil War service I will ever experience (or even wish to experience!). Our reenactment organization was invited to participate in the filming of Civil War battle scenes for Warner Brothers Films. The footage would be used in the award-winning television miniseries, "North and South," and scenes would also be stored in a film library for possible use in future movies. We joined approximately 1,400 other reenactors from across the nation on an isolated ranch near Natchez, Mississippi and for six days we experienced a virtual Civil War boot camp.

We soon discovered what we had gotten ourselves into. The first day we were marched two or three miles from camp to the Battle of Bull Run set where we found ourselves in the middle of an unbelievably real storm of battle. After about thirty minutes of innumerable explosions (including a two-story house blowing up), constant rifle fire, and frantic troop maneuvers, about 300 mounted Confederate cavalrymen were unleashed upon us. Some of them were in the same unit I used to ride with, Shelby's 5th Missouri Cavalry (reenactment units are frequently named after real historical army units). Those of us in the Union infantry were instructed to rout as the thundering herd reached our position. We had no problem obeying this order. Suddenly the art of acting came very naturally to us as our formation turned into a howling mob attempting to get out of the way of 300 stampeding horses. I "died" near an artillery piece, taking a nasty tumble that left my canteen mortally wounded and unable to hold water (I later purchased a replacement from the many "sutlers" that set up shop near our camp). The danger of battle seemed very real and when the

An ambulance removes a real casualty from the Battle of Bull Run set after he was trampled by a horse during the filming of "North and South." (Photo by Steve Cottrell)

guns fell silent and the smoke cleared, we discovered just how real it was: an ambulance crew lifted a Yank onto a stretcher, loaded him into their vehicle and drove away with flashing lights. He had been trampled by a horse. We were soon ordered back into formation to do the battle over again for a second time. During that memorable week, the routine removal of real casualties from various fields of battle became very common.

The scenes portraying the assault on the Confederate defenses at Petersburg, Virginia, produced more real casualties than any of the other footage shot that week near Natchez. Even a couple of the film's stars narrowly escaped serious injury in that wild hurly-burly. The actor who portrayed our brigadier general, James Read, experienced problems during the first charge we made. Upon reaching the enemy defenses, he stumbled and fell to the bottom of a seven-foot-deep trench, bending his steel sword and nearly knocking himself out. The rest of us had to go into that long, muddy trench also in order to claw our way to the top of the high dirt parapet where the Rebs waited for us. I recall seeing one Yank who had been knocked out cold by the blow of a rifle butt. Despite being in the middle of some wild hand-to-hand combat scenes with stuntmen, the well-known actor Patrick Swayze remained unscathed. However, another star who portrayed a sharpshooter officer, Parker Stevenson, had to be helped off the field after he was temporarily blinded by one of the numerous ground-charge explosions. The worst injury occurred when one Yank's rifle went off in his face and he lost an eye.

One of the highlights of that adventure in movie making occurred on the sixth day when we did some scenes with the respected actor Hal Holbrook, who portrayed President Lincoln. His stately demeanor and realistic appearance created the awesome feeling of being in the presence of the real Honest Abe himself.

Establishing a link with the past can certainly be exciting. Occasionally, however, incidents occur in the reenactment hobby when the past seems to actually transcend the present. Battlefield ghost stories are nothing new but encountering evidence of the spiritual world can certainly make one pause and wonder.

In the spring of 1983, I participated in an encampment at Wilson's Creek National Battlefield near Springfield, Missouri, where the second-largest battle of 1861 took place. During the weekend, a column of Union infantry reenactors was followed by a lone figure on horseback during a pre-dawn march. At least ten of the reenactors witnessed the solitary horseman slowly trailing them in the distance. Although his features were not clear, he appeared to be dressed in Civil War era clothing, including a wide-brimmed hat. At some point before the troops reached their destination, the horseman disappeared. Witnesses assumed the figure was merely a cavalry reenactor curious about their movements. When those of us in the only cavalry unit present at the event heard about the incident, we were quite surprised, since none of our members had been saddled that early in the morning. As far as we were able to determine, no one—reenactor, ranger, or visitor—was on horseback in the park at that time of the morning.

One night in December of 1984, I stood on the front lawn of the Borden House at Prairie Grove State Battlefield in Arkansas. Restless and unable to sleep, I was the last reenactor still awake after setting up camp late Friday night in preparation for that weekend's event. I had taken a stroll to the hill on which the historic old home stood, overlooking the valley from which Union troops assaulted Confederate positions on December 7, 1862. As I silently contemplated the history of the grounds on which I stood, I suddenly became aware of hundreds, maybe thousands, of voices in the distance. A football game was in progress somewhere down among the distant lights off to my right . . . I thought. Then I realized what time it was: between 1:00 and 2:00 A.M. There was certainly no sporting event taking place at that time of night, especially such a noisy one in a sparsely populated area. The distant roar of the crowd continued as I shook my head and paced back and forth. I finally relaxed and accepted it as reality. I remained on that hill for some time, listening to those disembodied voices.

The battlefield at Prairie Grove features a small souvenir shop in the park's museum where a number of postcards are available. Some of the cards feature scenes from reenactment events held at the site and one is a photo of a Confederate firing line kneeling behind a split-rail fence. Standing near the trees in the background of the picture, barely visible through the clouds of gunsmoke, are three lone figures in uniform. Strangely enough, no one in the reenactment organization has been able to identify these mysterious men whose ghostly images appear in the battlefield scene. As a matter of fact, no one can remember them being present when the photograph was taken!

A reenactment of part of the Battle of Prairie Grove. (Photo by Don Montgomery, courtesy of Prairie Grove Battlefield State Park)

In April 1989, on pasture land near McDonough, Georgia, outside of Atlanta, our reenactment organization was once again in the movie business. This time we filmed scenes portraying the Battle of Antietam for Tri-Star Pictures. The footage would be used in the Academy Award-winning motion picture *Glory*. As before, we were paid $50 a day, plus gas mileage, with free meals provided. For the weekend shoot, we camped in our usual reenactment manner: authentic-style canvas tents with straw for bedding. Bill Fannin (who had been our 1st sergeant during the 1984 live fire incident) was our unit's commanding officer during this expedition.

Rank positions in most reenactment units are the result of yearly elections as in other fraternal organizations such as the

Photo by Steve Cottrell

Elk's Club, etc. I have held rank four times during my reenactment service. The last couple of times I have been nominated, I have turned down the honor. As in most other fraternal groups, those who hold rank do most of the work and generally have the least fun. I much prefer the rank that legend says Davy Crockett chose in the Texas Revolution, "High Private."

The movie set included a perfect, full-scale replica of the Dunker Church, an historical structure present during the real 1862 battle in Maryland. The time and money which went into this building must have been significant, yet it was not used at all in a single scene in the finished movie. Once again, safety measures were not as high a priority on the film set as at a public reenactment. Unfortunately, the script called for a cavalry charge after we (the infantry) had been "shot up" and lay dangerously scattered about the area. The cavalry came galloping through and sure enough, one infantryman became a real casualty as a horse stomped on his head. Bleeding from his head wound, he was taken away in an ambulance for what appeared to be a fractured skull. I remember when they shot the scene over again right after this incident, I covered my head with my hands as the ground on which I was lying rumbled from the nearby stampede. Other casualties included two cavalrymen whose horses collided. One trooper was taken away in an ambulance after his mount rolled over on top of him. Ironically, the cavalry charge scene is shown for only about one second in the final film footage.

Well-known actors Matthew Broderick and Cary Elwes led us in numerous infantry charges against a long line of Confederates firing from behind a rail fence. Elwes suffered a minor wound when he accidentally sliced his hand open with his own sword during one of our wild assaults. The first aid crew wrapped his hand tightly in a flesh-colored bandage and we immediately shot the scene again. Elwes was frequently just a few feet in front of me leading us in bayonet charges. I recall when he looked directly at me with fire in his eyes and yelled "Come on!" during one attack. We all had to be careful to

134 CIVIL WAR IN TEXAS AND NEW MEXICO TERRITORY

dodge the numerous "flash pots" filled with gunpowder which simulated artillery shell explosions; they were going off everywhere around us during this scene.

A stunt man only two ranks behind me suffered a broken collar bone. He failed to land properly after being thrown ten feet or more into the air by a powerful springboard used to simulate the force of an explosion. His replacement cautioned us several times to be extra careful when we shot the scene again since his stunt required him to land between our ranks. He was afraid we might accidentally impale him with the steel bayonets fixed atop our rifles.

About fifty of us were involved in one close-up scene in which we got "shot up" in a gully. They did four takes of this scene. Unfortunately it wound up on the cutting room floor, like most of the footage they shot that weekend. It's difficult to see any of us as an individual in the finished movie. Everyone looks the same: hundreds of ugly, bearded guys in dusty uniforms running to and fro in the background of the scenes.

My only personal loss that wild weekend was my tin cup which normally dangles from my haversack whenever I participate in reenactment activities. By the end of Saturday, it was a badly misshapen mass of mangled metal because of the many falls I had taken. It fell to the ground, abandoned in that field in Georgia, where its rusty remains lay as a long-lost "war relic" of movie making.

Lately, fine quality educational films have been made using footage from large reenactments. I served on a Union artillery crew (with Bill Fannin and other ol' pards) at a national event held on the 130th anniversary of the Battle of Wilson's Creek, Missouri, in 1991, in which over five thousand reenactors participated. It was truly spectacular, with stark realism that is preserved on an excellent, informative videotape sold at Wilson's Creek National Battlefield. Likewise, another educational video, also with maps and narration, was made with scenes from the big 1995 reenactment of the Battle of Pea Ridge, Arkansas, where our infantry unit slogged through two days of mud and rain.

Speaking of Pea Ridge, one of the most uplifting experiences I ever had in the reenactment hobby took place Sunday morning on March 8, 1987, at Pea Ridge National Military Park. It was the 125th anniversary of the battle and I had the honor of delivering a devotional message for our camp's church service. I spoke from the historic porch of Elkhorn Tavern on that hallowed field that was so crucial to the outcome of the war in the Trans-Mississippi Theater. This was the battlefield where the great Texan hero, Gen. Ben McCulloch, was killed in action along with many brave men on both sides. The Pea Ridge encampment was an event I helped to arrange with park personnel and unit leaders. Since that time, the park has held an encampment every year.

I have participated in innumerable events during my "tour of duty" in reenactment. Some were hot as blazes, such as the Battle of Honey Springs, Oklahoma, in 1996 where the temperature reached 103 degrees, and some were nearly freezing, such as the Battle of Prairie Grove, Arkansas, in 1982, with gray December clouds spitting snow. Some were large extravaganzas with many units and hordes of spectators, like the Battle of Brice's Crossroads, Mississippi, in 1984. Others were small but very unique, like the wagon train massacre at Baxter Springs, Kansas, in 1985. But some were just tiny skirmishes that seemed trifling at the time, such as the 125th anniversary of the Battle of Carthage, Missouri, on July 5, 1986, in which I had the honor of commanding the entire Union force (just a squad of eight infantrymen). I recall how I deployed my troops in a defiant firing line that spanned the width of the dusty farm road on the actual site of Colonel Franz Sigel's masterful fighting retreat in 1861. Our color bearer waved Old Glory proudly in the hot summer air as we held off a small but menacing force of Rebel reenactors who were supported by a noisy little howitzer. We marched and volleyed for miles before finally breaking contact with the "enemy" and entering town for the final ceremonies.

As it turned out, our minor skirmish at Carthage received excellent publicity thanks to the help of a local journalist and

Photo by Bob Tommey

historian, Mr. Marvin VanGilder. By the power of the press, our sweaty little march was transformed into a major local news story that attracted the attention of many people. Less than a year later, that dusty road on which we trod received an important new designation. With the help of Mr. VanGilder and County Commissioner Danny Hensley, old County Road Number 15 was officially renamed "Civil War Road" and handsome road signs bearing the new name were installed. The pathway of history was marked for posterity.

Civil War Road is not far from my house. Whenever I pass that way, I am reminded of how a determined force of reenactors, with a pitifully small amount of troops and firepower, marched in the steps of their predecessors and succeeded in

Steve Cottrell. (Photo by Bob Tommey)

preserving a piece of our heritage in the mind of the public. Also I think about reenactors who are still "refighting" the war and keeping our history alive. I hope they win their fight . . . it is a noble cause.

Bibliography

Brownlee, Richard S. *Gray Ghosts of the Confederacy.* Baton Rouge, LA: Louisiana State University Press, 1958.

Cottrell, Steve. *Civil War in the Indian Territory.* Gretna, LA: Pelican Publishing Company, 1995.

Davis, Edwin Adams. *Fallen Guidon: The Saga of Confederate General Jo Shelby's March to Mexico.* College Station, TX: Texas A & M University Press, 1995.

Foote, Shelby. *The Civil War: A Narrative.* Volume I. New York: Random House, 1974.

Frazier, Donald S. *Blood and Treasure: Confederate Empire in the Southwest.* College Station, TX: Texas A & M University Press, 1995.

Gallaway, B. P., ed. *Texas, The Dark Corner of the Confederacy: Contemporary Accounts of the Lone Star State in the Civil War.* Lincoln, NB: University of Nebraska Press, 1994.

Gowan, Hugh and Judy. *Stories, Anecdotes, and Humor From the Civil War.* Martinsburg, PA: Daisy Publications, 1983.

Hall, Martin H. *Sibley's New Mexico Campaign.* Austin, TX: University of Texas Press, 1960.

Josephy, Alvin M. *The Civil War in the American West.* New York: Alfred A. Knopf, Inc., 1991.

Josephy, Alvin M. and the Editors of Time-Life Books. *War on the Frontier: The Trans-Mississippi West.* Alexandria, VA: Time-Life Books, Inc., 1986.

Kurtz, Henry I. "Last Battle of the War." *Civil War Times Illustrated.* Vol. I, No. 1, April 1962. Gettysburg, PA: 1962.

Miller, Edward Stokes. *Civil War Sea Battles.* Conshohocken, PA: Combined Books, Inc., 1995.

Page, Dave. *Ships Versus Shore: Civil War Engagements Along Southern Shores and Rivers.* Nashville, TN: Rutledge Hill Press, 1994.

Porter, David D. *The Naval History of the Civil War.* Secaucus, NJ: Castle, 1984.

Reader's Digest Assn. *America's Fascinating Indian Heritage.* Pleasantville, NY: The Reader's Digest Association, 1978.

Steele, Phillip W. *Starr Tracks: Belle and Pearl Starr.* Gretna, LA: Pelican Publishing Company, 1992.

Steele, Phillip and Cottrell, Steve. *Civil War in the Ozarks.* Gretna, LA: Pelican Publishing Company, 1993.

Trudeau, Noah Andre. *Out of the Storm: The End of the Civil War, April-June 1865.* Boston: Little, Brown and Company, 1994.

Tyson, Carl Newton. "Texas: Men for War; Cotton for Economy." *Journal of the West.* Vol. XIV, No. 1, January 1975. Los Angeles, CA: Lorrin L. Morrison and Carroll Spear Morrison, 1975.

Wheeler, Keith and the Editors of Time-Life Books. *The Scouts.* Alexandria, VA: Time-Life Books Inc., 1978.

Index to Battles
and Skirmishes